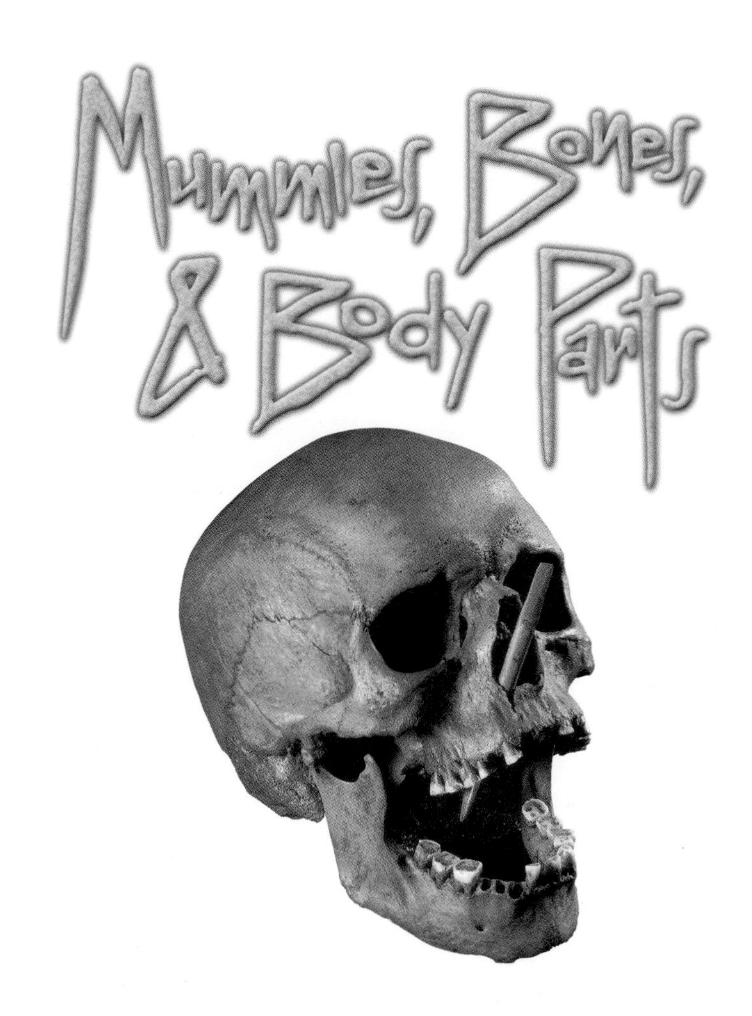
Mummies, Bones, & Body Parts

CHARLOTTE WILCOX

SCHOLASTIC INC.
New York Toronto London Auckland Sydney
Mexico City New Delhi Hong Kong Buenos Aires

Front cover: *A young girl from the Inca empire of Peru, who was sacrificed on a mountaintop five hundred years ago, stares across time.*
Back cover: *The mummy of the Egyptian king Seti I*
Page one: *A human skull, pierced by an arrow, tells a story of a violent end.*
Page two: *From piles of bones and other remains, like these found in Peru, scientists piece together clues about how people lived and died in the past.*
Opposite page: *The dead tell many tales. These people lived in Chile, where the dry heat of the desert preserved their bodies.*

ISBN 0-439-32335-5

Published by Scholastic Inc., 555 Broadway, New York, NY 10012,
by arrangement with Lerner Publications Company, a division of Lerner Publishing Group.

12 11 10 9 8 7 6 5 4 3 1 2 3 4 5 6/0

Printed in the U.S.A. 08

First Scholastic printing, October 2001

CONTENTS

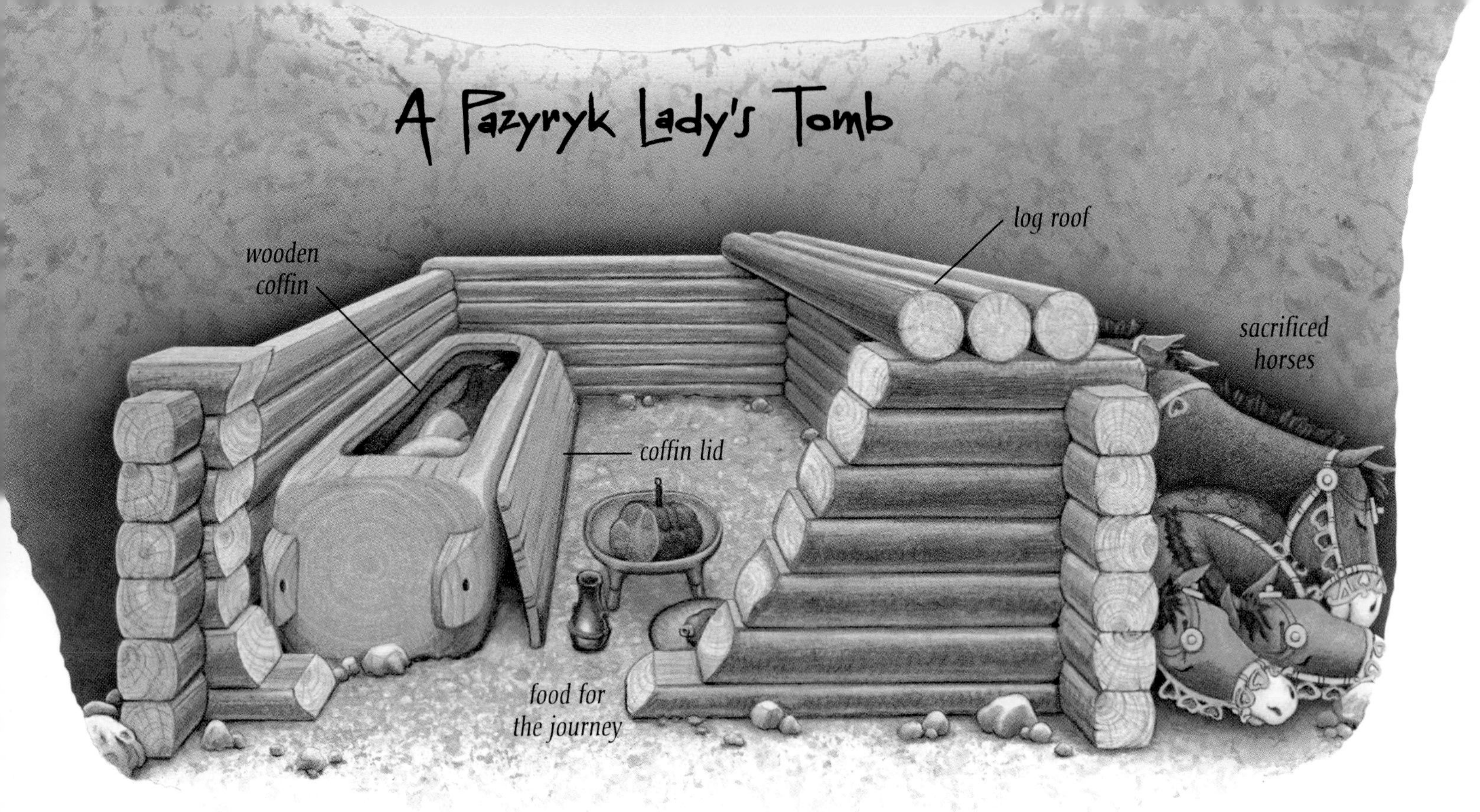

Chapter 1

THE LONG REST

A lovely young lady died about 2,400 years ago. She was a noblewoman from a tribe called the Pazyryk. They raised horses and sheep in the mountains where Russia, China, and Mongolia meet.

The woman was only about twenty-five years old when she died. But she held an important position in her community. Her death brought sadness to the whole tribe. The Pazyryk believed the young woman's soul would travel to a beautiful mountain grassland far away. But her body was still with them. They worked together to care for it.

The Pazyryk people of Asia believed the souls of the dead could travel to another land. They treated the dead with great respect and care. The log-lined tomb (cross section opposite page and left) *of a Pazyryk woman who died some 2,400 years ago contained everything, including good riding horses, that the woman would need on her journey to another life.*

PREPARING FOR BURIAL

The woman died in winter, when it was impossible to dig a grave in the frozen ground. Her relatives had to keep her body until spring. They cut out the softest parts (organs and muscles) because these would decay the fastest. They filled the body with fur and spices. They dressed the lady in her best clothes—striped wool skirt, silk top, braided belt, and high riding boots. They fixed her hair with a three-foot-high, gold-covered hairpiece. Then they wrapped her in a fur blanket.

Men from the tribe traveled fifteen miles on horseback to the forest. They cut down a tree to build the coffin. It had to be nearly eight feet long because of the woman's tall hairpiece. When the ground was soft, the men dug a gigantic hole in the earth. In the bottom, they built a room with log walls.

THE FUNERAL

By late June, everything was ready for the funeral. The body was carefully laid in the coffin. The woman's family placed some of her belongings inside—a mirror, dishes, and beads. Then they nailed the lid shut and lowered the coffin into the deep grave.

Finally, the woman's most valuable treasures were buried with her—six horses, all dressed in gold-covered harnesses. The Pazyryk needed good horses to live in the mountains. They believed the lady would also need horses after death. The horses were led to the edge of the hole. A man hit each horse very hard in the forehead with an ax. Then the horses were lowered into the hole.

A roof of logs was placed over the burial room. All the dirt was pushed back into the hole. Then it was covered with a pile of rocks several feet high. The woman's relatives were satisfied that they had given her a safe place to start her journey to another life. They thought her body would rest in peace.

Not long after the funeral, rain or melted snow filled the burial room. It soon froze, sealing the coffin in a block of ice. A few years later, another tribe uncovered the grave and buried a man in it. The woman was not disturbed. Her body remained safe in the ice-filled grave. Some time later, robbers dug into the grave. But once again the woman was not disturbed.

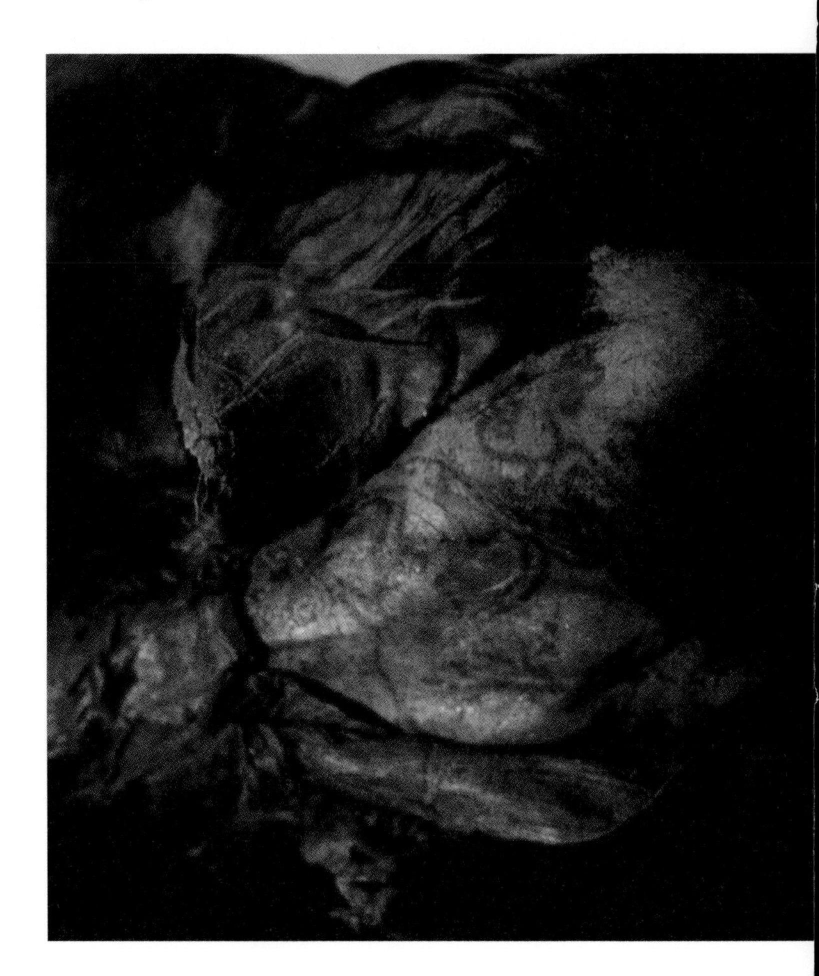

Some of the earliest tattoos ever recorded cover the noblewoman's body.

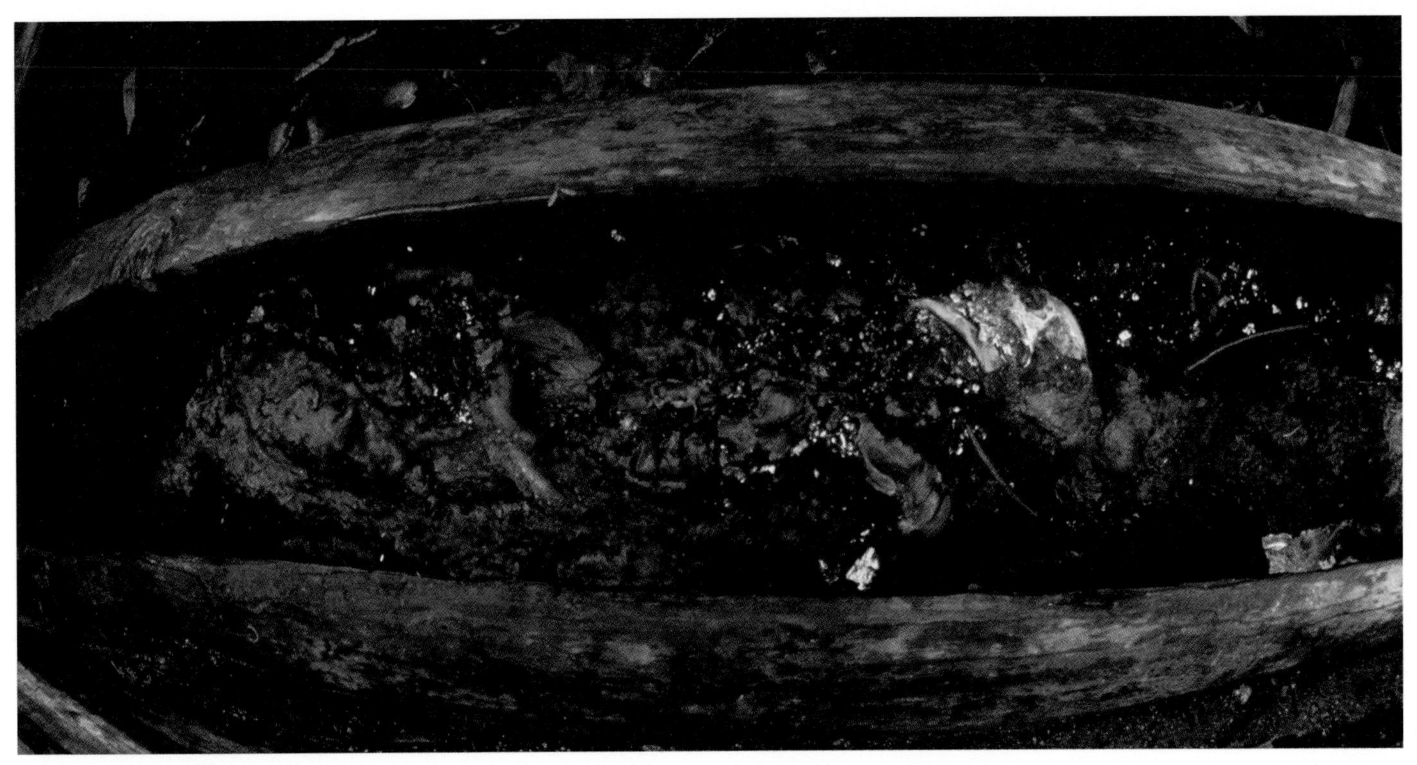

The woman's tomb, frozen in ice for thousands of years, was carefully thawed by scientists who discovered it in 1993.

A MUMMY IS FOUND

In 1993, Russian scientist Natalia Polosmak brought a team of researchers to the mountains. They wanted to learn more about the Pazyryk people. Under hundreds of pounds of dirt and rocks, they found a grave. In the bottom was the woman's coffin still sealed with nails pounded in by her relatives.

After days of slowly melting the ice, scientists uncovered the woman's body. Her once beautiful face was mostly bones, but the rest of her body was well preserved. The scientists had mixed feelings about what they were doing. Some even had nightmares. After taking the body away for study, they sent it back to a museum near the mountain where the woman had lived and died. She is close to the place where her family buried her, but far from the peaceful rest they tried to provide.

A graveyard is a place where the bodies of the dead are put to rest. Graveyards are frightening places to some people, sacred to others, and sad places to most everyone.

LOOKING AFTER THE DEAD

When people die, they leave their bodies behind. The living are left to care for the dead. Caring for the dead has been an important part of human life throughout history.

Seeing the body of a loved one decay is disturbing. For this reason, bodies are usually placed out of sight fairly soon after death. Some societies place their dead high in special trees where no one is allowed to look. Others send dead bodies far out to sea in funeral boats. Some bodies are cremated, or burned to ashes.

The most common way of caring for the dead all over the world is burial. Everyone knows the body will decay, but no one sees it. For thousands of years, human bodies have been buried in the ground, in caves, or in special burial houses. Scientists can only guess how many billions of people have been buried on our planet.

Ways of caring for the dead are as varied as the people of the earth. The Crow Indians of North America traditionally placed their dead on platforms high in tree branches.

Most bodies that are buried begin to decay very soon. Decay is caused by bacteria and fungi that grow in the dead body and eat the tissues, beginning just a few hours after death. Within a day or two, decay causes the body to change color and give off an odor. After a few weeks, the softest parts of the body begin to be eaten away. Within a few years, all the soft tissue (skin, muscles, and organs) is completely eaten up, with only bones left behind.

STOPPING DECAY

In some cultures, dead bodies are embalmed before burial. Embalming preserves the dead body from decay, sometimes for only a short time, sometimes for many centuries. People all over the world have embalmed the dead for thousands of years. In modern North America, most embalming is intended to last only a few days, until the funeral takes place. Then the body is buried and begins to decay.

Some ancient cultures used embalming to preserve dead bodies from *ever* decaying. In places like Egypt and the Inca empire of South America, they were very successful. Millions of bodies have been preserved for thousands of years in those regions. Preserved bodies are called mummies.

Many mummified bodies have been found in Egypt, a place where embalming and burial were highly developed in ancient times.

WHAT MAKES A MUMMY?

In a mummy, some or all of the soft tissue does not decay after death. This happens when the bacteria and fungi that cause decay cannot grow in the dead body. Some mummies are preserved from decay by embalming. Others are preserved by natural conditions where the body is placed.

Mummification happens most often when the body dries out quickly after death, because bacteria and fungi need water to live. A body placed in the sun or in hot, dry sand may turn into a mummy. A body embalmed with chemicals, fire, or smoke (removing all water from the tissues soon after death) may become a mummy too.

Mummification also happens when a body is quickly and permanently frozen soon after death, because most bacteria cannot grow in below-freezing temperatures. Some mummies are buried in soil containing chemicals that kill bacteria, or in caves that contain gases that kill bacteria. A body will also become a mummy if all air is taken away from it, since bacteria and fungi need air as well as water to grow. Bodies sealed in airtight coffins have been preserved in this way.

Not all mummies are created on purpose. Some just happen. This person's body dried out quickly and thoroughly in the hot desert air of Chile, creating mummified remains.

New Ways to Make Mummies

Modern scientists have developed new ways to preserve bodies, creating modern mummies. One method is called cryonics. Cryonics is the practice of freezing a body in hopes of bringing the person back to life in the future. Usually the goal is to freeze the body until a cure is found for the disease that caused the person's death.

Bodies preserved in this way must be specially treated right after death. Blood must be removed and replaced with a special substance similar to what is used to preserve organs for transplantation. The body is then frozen at an extremely low temperature–lower than three hundred degrees Fahrenheit below zero. This is done by placing the body in a large container filled with liquid nitrogen.

The first person ever to be preserved by cryonics was James Bedford, who died of cancer in 1967. His frozen body is stored at a cryonics facility near Phoenix, Arizona. Many other people since then have had their bodies frozen at death.

No one knows if they will ever be revived. Scientists have only been successful in reviving animals frozen for just a few hours. Even so, people and their families continue to spend $30,000 to $120,000 for cryonic storage. They have the same hopes the ancient Egyptians had, that preserving the body will allow them to walk and talk with their loved ones again someday.

Hoping that scientists will someday be able to reverse death and cure all diseases, some people have chosen to have their remains or the remains of loved ones placed in cryonic storage. Two members of the same family are preserved in this container in Arizona.

The hardest part of the human body to destroy, bones are also the most common form of human remains available for study.

THE BITS WE LEAVE BEHIND

Most bodies don't become mummies. But they still leave evidence behind. Bacteria and fungi cannot eat bone. The skeleton is the longest-lasting part of the body. Human bones have survived being burned, cut in pieces, crushed, and dissolved with chemicals. Bones can last for centuries after the bodies they once wore have completely disappeared.

Anything that is left of a human body is called the remains. This can be an entire preserved body, body parts, bones, or ashes. Bones are the most common form of human remains. Skeletons, bones, and bone fragments are found anyplace in the world where humans have died.

Most people expect that, after burial, their bodies will remain unseen and untouched. But this does not always happen. Bodies and bones are unearthed for many reasons. Scientists find bodies while looking for human remains to study. Grave robbers hunting for treasures to sell may dig bodies up in ancient burial grounds. Other bodies are dug up accidentally, when people build new roads or plow new fields.

Paleopathologists sometimes study teeth and bones as well as soft tissues for clues about health, diet, and nutrition in the past.

STUDYING HUMAN REMAINS

Whenever a human body, body part, or bone is found, someone has to study it. Did the person die by accident or has a crime been committed? When did the person die and who was he or she? Many different kinds of scientists work to draw the answers out of bodies and bones.

Forensic anthropologists study recent human remains to solve crimes or settle disputes in court. Even tiny fragments of human tissue, hair, or bone can give them important clues.

Physical anthropologists study ancient human remains, most often skeletons and bones. If the body is ancient, an archaeologist may also be called in to examine the place where the body was found. Archaeologists investigate the past by studying artifacts (such as clothing, tools, and artworks), buildings, ancient writing, and other objects.

Paleopathologists also examine ancient human remains, especially the preserved soft tissues of mummies. Paleopathologists study diseases, health, and nutrition of the past. They use some of the same methods modern doctors use on living people to answer questions about how humans lived long, long ago.

These scientists study human history from different angles. Without human remains to study, forensic anthropologists, physical anthropologists, and paleopathologists would be unable to do their jobs. Bodies or skeletons—sometimes even small pieces of them—can tell scientists whether people were male or female and how old they were at death. Human remains hold clues about how people lived and how they died.

Many of the photographs in this book show human remains. Some are disturbing or even shocking. Most are of specimens that are already on display in a museum or school. Many of the photographs point out the importance of human remains to science and education. But human remains are often handled or kept in disrespectful ways. A few of the photographs in this book are included to show how *not* to treat the dead. In all cases, these mummies, bones, and body parts should be viewed with respect.

Archaeologists study ancient people, their cultures and their artifacts. Here an archaeologist uncovers the coffin of an Egyptian mummy.

The age of this well-preserved body, found in a peat bog in Ireland in the late 1970s, remains a mystery to scientists.

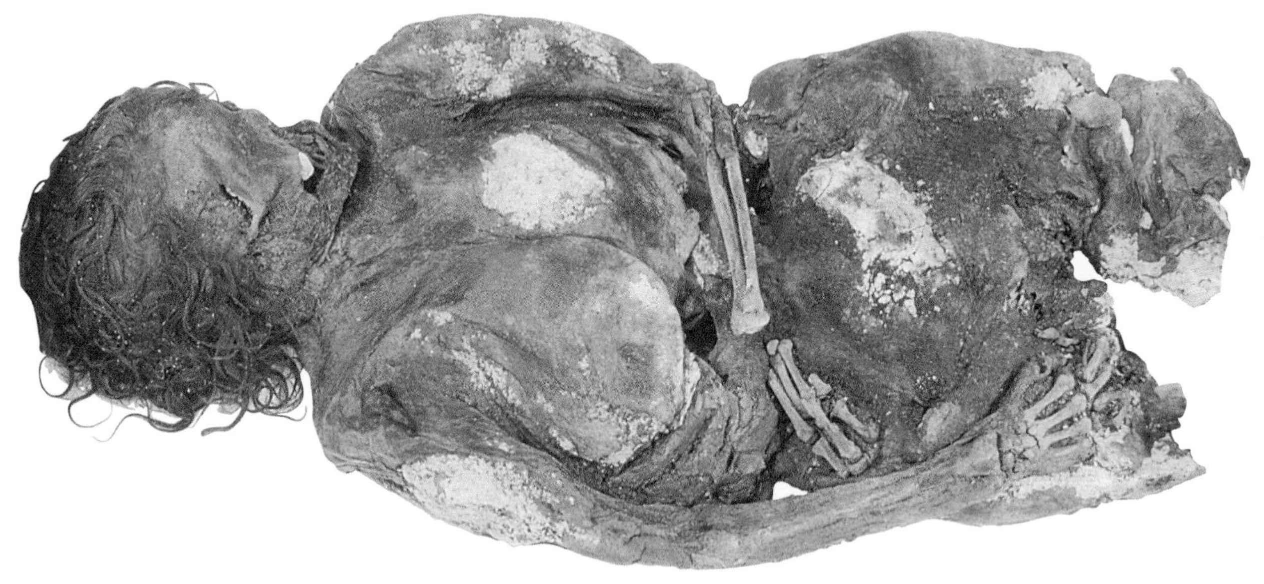

Chapter 3

HOW OLD ARE THEY?

One of the first things scientists try to find out about remains is how old they are. Did the person die recently or a long time ago? Scientists look at three things to decide how old human remains are: the location of the remains, the things found with the body or bones, and the remains themselves.

THE WOMAN IN THE BOG

Nearly fifteen hundred preserved bodies have turned up in peat bogs in northern Europe over the years. Some may be up to three thousand years old. Acids in the soil of peat bogs keep bacteria from growing, turning bodies into mummies. Meenybraddan Woman is a mummified body found in a peat bog in Ireland in the late 1970s.

Investigators looked first at the area where Meenybraddan Woman was found for clues about her age. How deep was the body buried? What was on top of it and around it? What changes could be seen in the soil between the body and the surface? How long did it take for these changes to occur? The place where Meenybraddan Woman was found had been disturbed by people digging peat, so scientists used other tools to determine her age.

They studied items found with the body, such as clothing. When experts examined Meenybraddan Woman's woolen cloak, they found it was a style worn from the late 1500s to the late 1600s.

Scientists also studied Meenybraddan Woman's body for clues. Some of her preserved tissue was tested using radiocarbon dating. This is a way of finding the age of old material by measuring how much carbon it contains. Radiocarbon dating can only be done on something that was once alive, such as human or animal tissue, plant material, and artifacts made from plants, skins, bone, hair, or feathers. Meenybraddan Woman's body was radiocarbon dated to about A.D. 1200.

How old was the body? Studying the clothes gave one answer, while dating the tissue gave another. Both methods are considered good ways to date a body, but in the case of Meenybraddan Woman at least one of them must be wrong.

Radiocarbon dating measures the amount of a radioactive form of carbon (carbon 14) contained in human or other once living remains. Measuring how much carbon 14 is still in remains gives scientists a good guess at their age. Here, a lab worker prepares a sample for dating.

This skull, pulled from a peat bog in England, solved a crime but left many questions unanswered.

THE LINDOW MUMMY MURDER MYSTERY

Some scientists question the accuracy of radiocarbon dating. Mummies found in Lindow Moss, a peat bog near Cheshire, England, show why. Workers digging in the bog found a human head in 1983. They took it to the police. The police thought the head belonged to a local woman who had been missing since 1960. The woman's husband, who lived next to the bog, had always said he did not know what happened to his wife.

The police told the husband they now had his wife's head, pulled from the bog. The husband then confessed that he had killed his wife, cut her body into pieces, and buried it in the bog. He was sentenced to prison for murder.

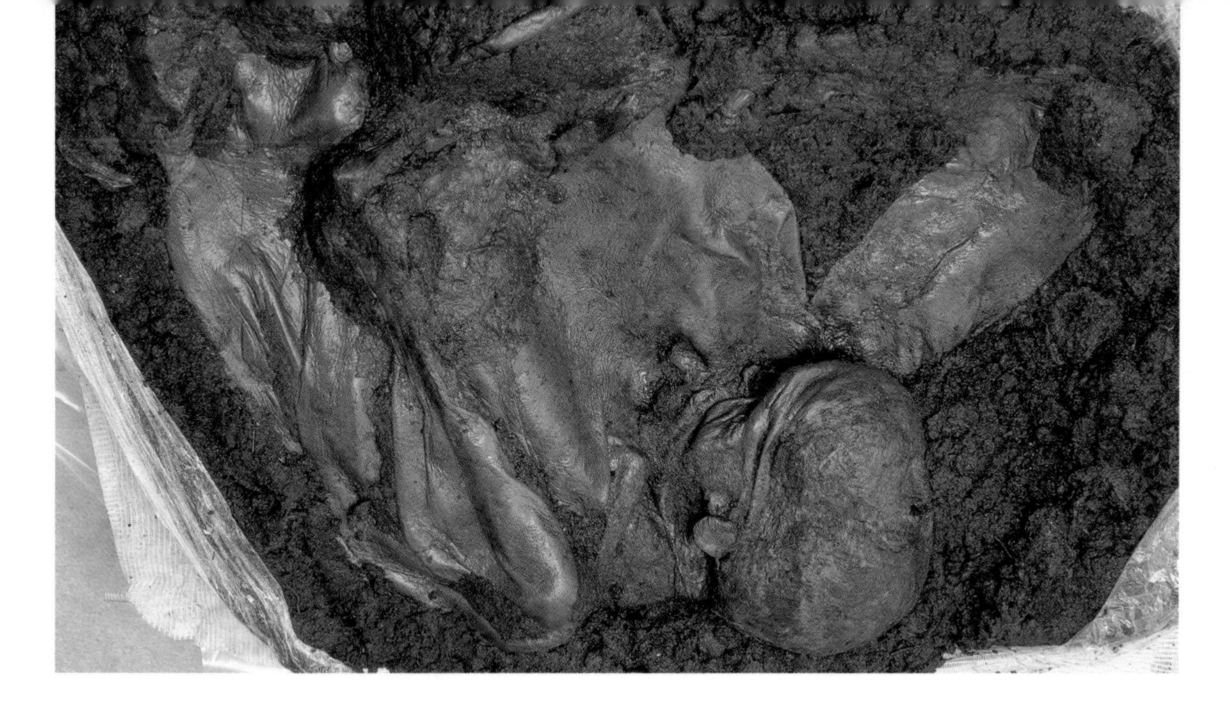

Clues to the age of Lindow II were found in his mouth, where no evidence of fillings or other modern dental work could be found.

The husband said he buried all the body parts. But in spite of much digging, no more human remains were found. One police inspector had doubts about the head. So he ordered radiocarbon dating and was told the head was almost two thousand years old! That left the police with a confessed murderer, and no body at all. Scientists named the head Lindow I.

The case took a different turn the next summer. The same crew working in Lindow Moss found part of a right leg and foot. This time they called an archaeologist, Rick Turner. He began digging in the bog and found the complete top half of a body. The bottom half was missing, except for the lower right leg and foot the workers had found first.

Although Turner suspected the body was ancient, he asked the police to take a look. Some police investigators thought the body might belong to the murdered wife. The body came to be known as Lindow II.

The first hint that Lindow II was very old came from X rays. X rays showed not even one filling in the full set of teeth. This convinced Turner and other scientists that the body was not modern. Almost all modern bodies have some metal fillings in the teeth. But the police were not convinced.

Scientists work together to preserve, clean, and study the remains of Lindow II. Newspaper reporters nicknamed the man "Pete Moss," after his burial place, the English peat bog known as Lindow Moss.

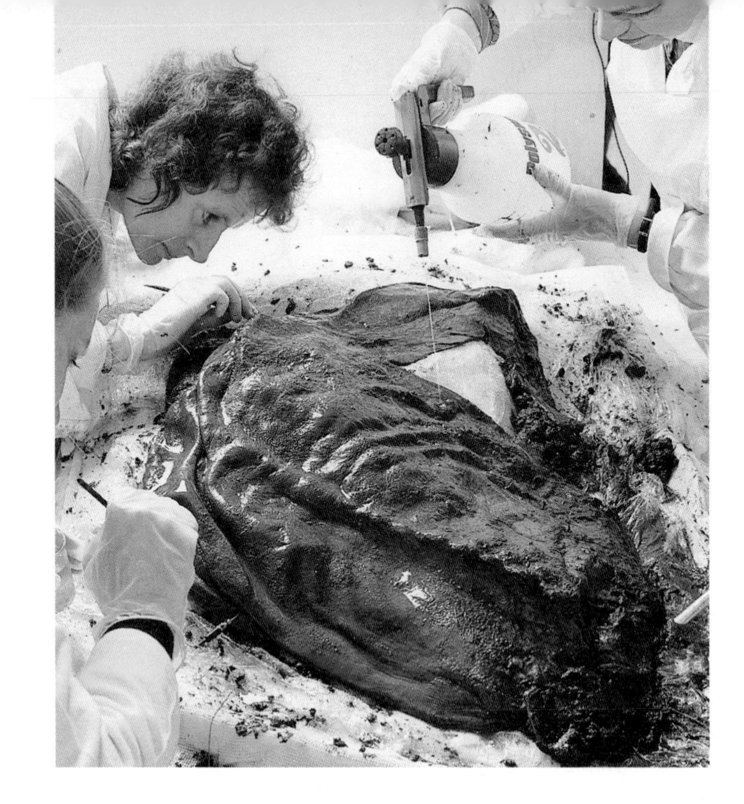

Turner had the body radiocarbon dated. The first report said Lindow II was at least 1,000 years old. Later the same laboratory dated the body at about 1,500 years. A second laboratory dated Lindow II at about 2,000 years old. Yet another laboratory showed the age to be about 1,650 years old. This led some police researchers to claim the radiocarbon tests could not be trusted.

Skeptical police looked once again at the head of Lindow I. They sent it to Peter Vanezis, a famous forensic pathologist. He studied features of the head and compared it to photos of the missing woman. Vanezis, who distrusts radiocarbon dating, believes the skull could be that of the murdered wife.

In 1987, more body parts turned up in Lindow Moss. This body was called Lindow III. It was accidentally cut in pieces by digging machinery. Even so, the entire body was recovered, except for the head. Did this body belong to the head known as Lindow I? At first, some scientists thought so. Later tests showed that the head belonged to a woman, while the remains known as Lindow III belonged to a man.

Almost a year and a half later more human remains were found. They included a right thigh and part of a left leg. Most scientists think these are not a separate body but the missing parts of Lindow II.

Were there two, three, or even four bodies in the bog? Are they one thousand years old, two thousand years old, or somewhere in between? Or is one a modern murder victim? New research methods may answer these questions in the future.

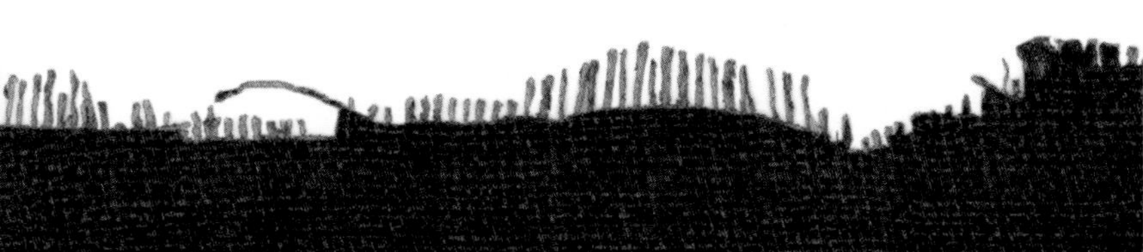

This hat, found with a mummified body in a glacier in Canada and carbon dated to be about 550 years old, looks surprisingly modern.

Canada's Iceman

In the summer of 1999, three hunters were hiking through a park reserve in northwest British Columbia, Canada, near where Alaska, British Columbia, and Yukon Territory meet. On the edge of a glacier, the hunters made a grisly discovery—a human body sticking out of the ice.

Because the body was found on land controlled by native peoples called the Champagne and Aishihik First Nations, a team of scientists and Indian leaders went to the park to investigate. They found the body still frozen and took it to a museum for preservation.

At the museum, clothing and artifacts found with the body were radiocarbon dated and found to be about 550 years old. Scientists agree that Canada's Iceman lived before Europeans came to the region, and scientists and First Nations people hope that further study of his body will yield clues about how life was lived long ago. Indians have named the area where the man was found Kwaday Dän Sinchi, which means "Long Ago Person Found."

WHAT KILLED THEM?

After determining the age of human remains, scientists often next look to see how a person died. Murder, disease, and accidents leave traces behind on skin, bone, and body parts. But those traces may be hard to see with the naked eye.

THE PAST UNDER A MICROSCOPE

Much of medical research is done under a microscope. Scientists usually place a thin slice of tissue on a glass slide. But most mummies are too dry and brittle to slice. Scientists must rehydrate the tissues so they can be studied. Rehydrating puts water back into the tissues. It is often done by soaking the tissues in human blood serum. This is the clear, thin, liquid part of blood.

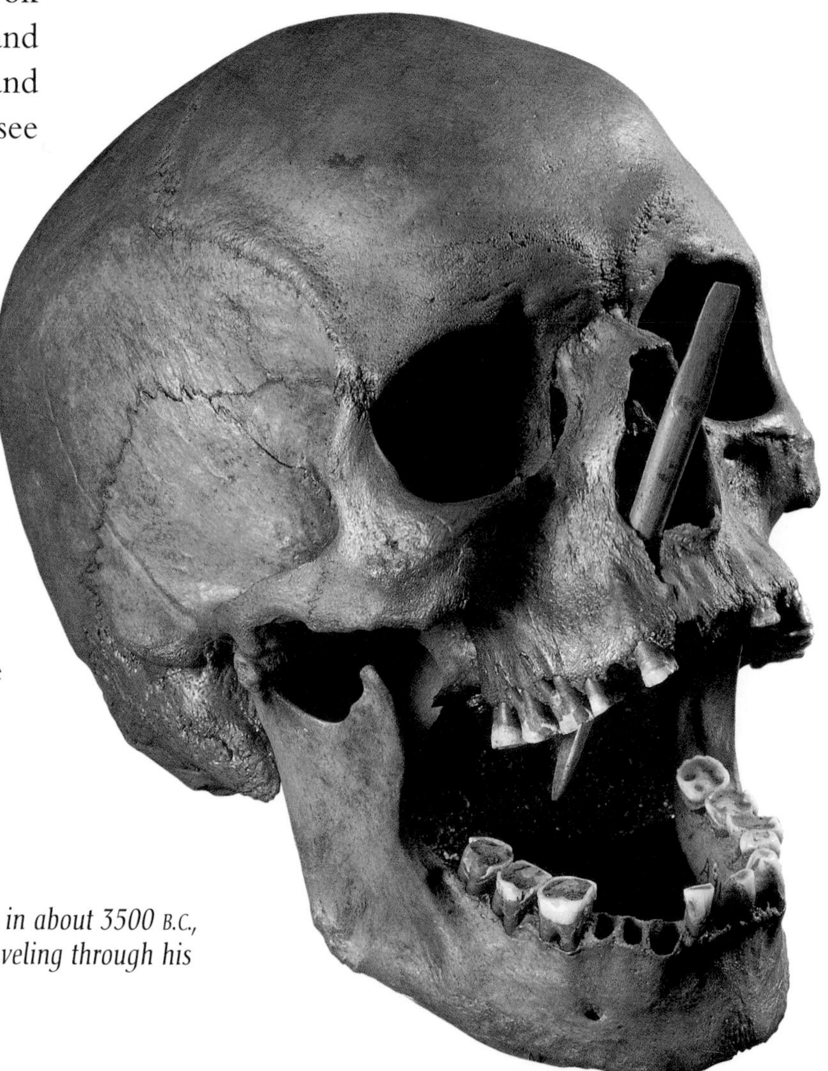

Sometimes, the cause of death seems clear. This man died in about 3500 B.C., but not from the wound to his head. Instead, an arrow traveling through his breastbone pierced a major artery.

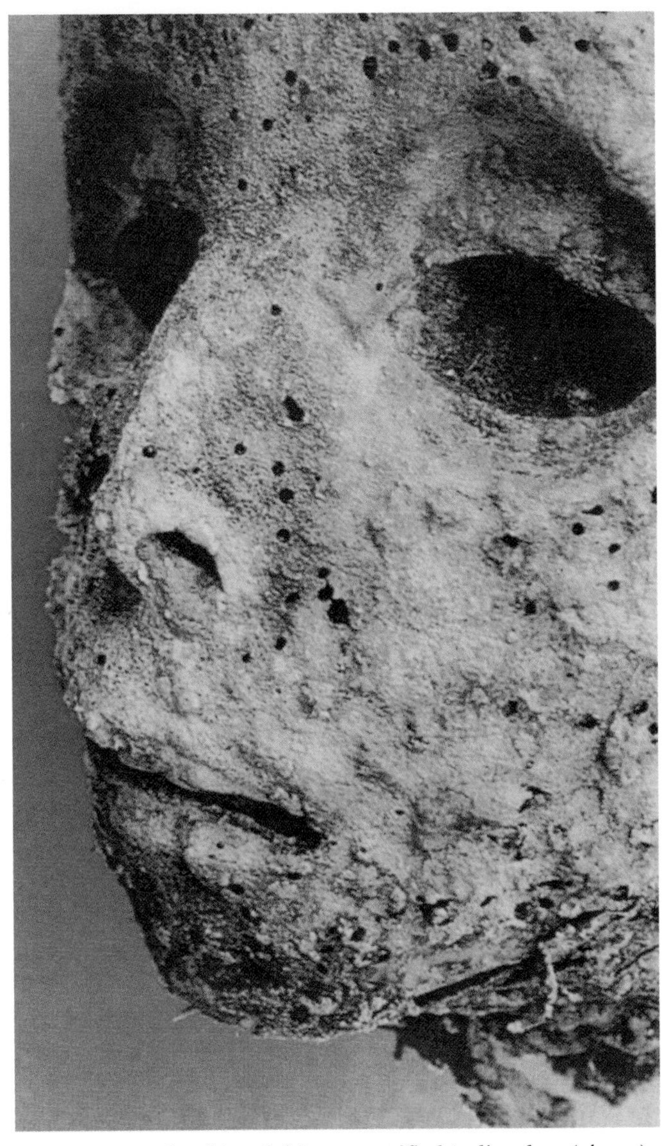

Tiny scars on the skin of this mummified Italian boy (above) *led scientists to believe he died of smallpox. Tissue from mummies* (above, right) *is sometimes so dry that moisture, in the form of blood serum, must be added to it before it can be studied.*

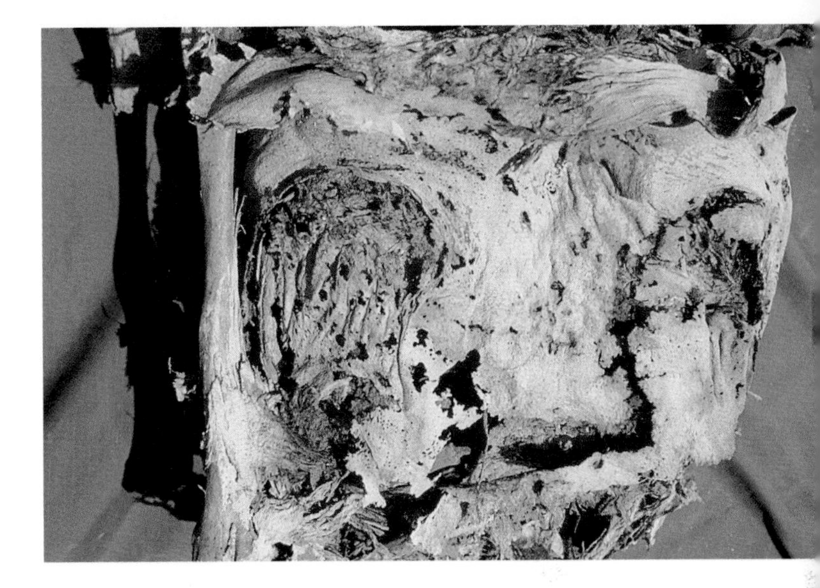

Researchers studied the body of a two-year-old boy from Naples, Italy, in this way. The boy died about four hundred years ago. He must have come from a well-to-do family, because he was buried in an expensive coffin in an important church. When scientists uncovered his mummified body and saw his face, they suspected he died of smallpox. Pimplelike scars are typical of this very contagious disease.

Researchers soaked some of the scarred tissue in serum. Looking at it under a microscope, they saw evidence of the virus that causes smallpox. Without this microscopic evidence, they might have guessed why he died but would not have known for sure.

Along with studying tissues under a microscope, scientists sometimes do autopsies to examine mummies and other remains. An autopsy is a medical examination of a dead person. It involves cutting open the dead body and examining the organs and fluids within. In modern medicine, an autopsy is usually done to find out the cause of death, or occasionally to identify the person. With old or ancient remains, researchers look for much more than what killed a person.

The well-preserved bodies of Philip Calvert, his wife, and a baby were found in a Maryland cornfield in 1990. Historians knew that Calvert was governor of the colony of Maryland in 1660 and 1661. The Calverts were well off for their time, but autopsies showed signs of a hard life.

The baby died of infection in the brain and spine. Governor Calvert had been in poor health. He died, possibly from a heart attack, at about age fifty. His wife died at about age fifty-five after much suffering. Her teeth and bones were in very poor condition, probably from lack of good nutrition. A broken leg had never healed and was infected. The Calvert mummies show that life in Colonial America, even for the well-to-do, was not easy.

Burial in a lead coffin preserved the bones, hair, and some of the soft tissue of this woman from Colonial Maryland. Since the carbon content of bones varies according to how much corn a person has eaten, scientists could tell that the woman was not born in the New World, where corn is commonly eaten, but had lived there for several years.

Top: *X rays of this Egyptian mummy's head revealed that eight of the man's molars were missing.*

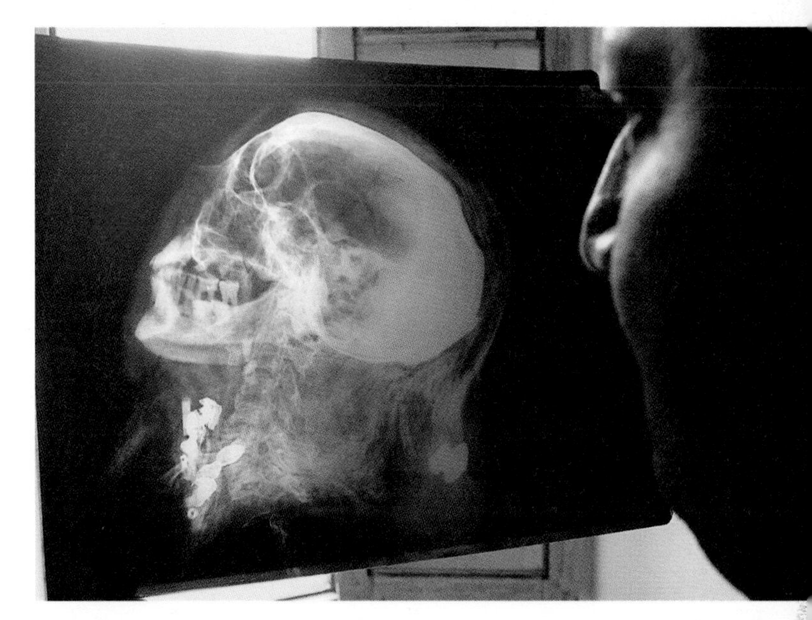

TAKING PICTURES OF BONES

Autopsies and studies of tissue under a microscope can answer many questions about how and why people died in the past. But these methods involve cutting the dead body and removing tissue. X rays allow scientists to look inside bodies such as mummies without disturbing them.

X rays are helping scientists determine how the oldest known European died. In 1991, hikers came across a frozen body in the high Alps near the border between Austria and Italy. It is among the oldest and best-preserved mummies in the world.

The mummy is called the Iceman because his body was frozen for nearly five thousand years. He died in the mountains with no one to care for his dead body. A glacier covered him soon after death.

Right: *The oldest known European, known as the Iceman, lay undisturbed on a mountaintop for five thousand years until two hikers discovered his body in 1991.*

The Iceman brought many questions to scientists. Why did he die alone in the mountains? Where did he come from? Archaeologist Konrad Spindler headed the search to answer these questions. Spindler and other scientists looked at the Iceman's body, clothing, and the things he carried with him.

THE ICEMAN

By studying the body, scientists found that the Iceman had not been eating well. He had used up nearly all of his body fat. X rays showed broken ribs that had not healed. The Iceman had not been using his right arm for at least two or three weeks. Though the arm was not broken, scientists believe moving it made his ribs hurt.

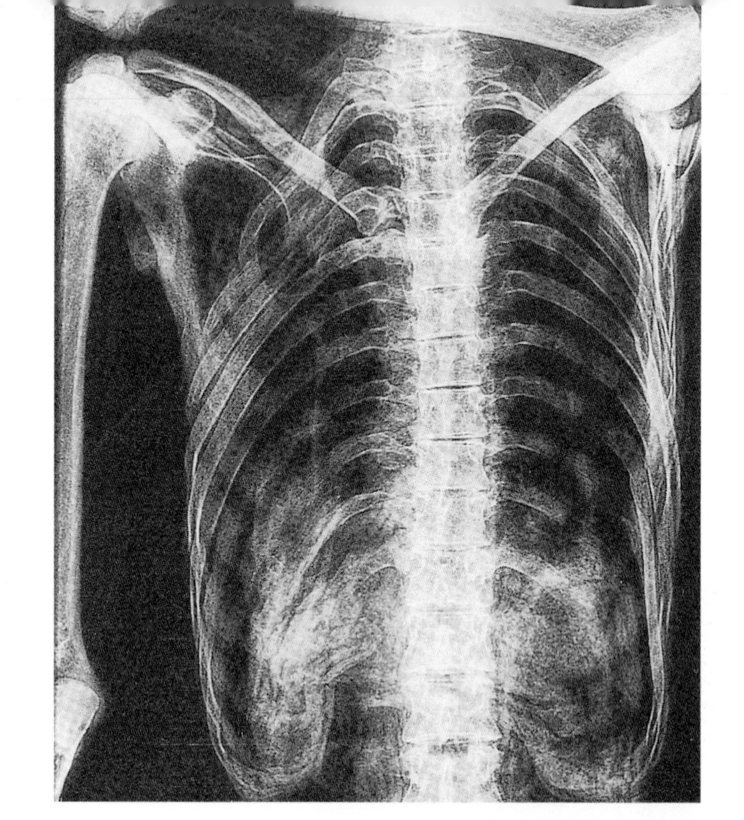

A possible cause of death for the Iceman emerged when scientists read his chest X rays (top). *Broken ribs had not healed and may have made him unable to gather food. Hungry and cold in his grass cape* (right), *the Iceman became too weak to travel.*

Among the things the Iceman carried were a copper ax with a wood handle, a flint knife in a case, an unfinished bow, and a quiver with two broken arrows and some unfinished arrows. The only food he had with him was a piece of dried meat and one small piece of fruit. Because this type of fruit does not ripen until late fall, scientists could pinpoint the time of year the Iceman had died. But this brought up more questions. Why did the Iceman go alone into the mountains with winter coming on? Why was his food almost gone?

Researchers found pieces of grain in the Iceman's clothes. This showed he had been below the mountain in fields planted with grain not long before his death. But his equipment was that of a mountain man, not a farmer. Maybe he was a shepherd who lived in a village below the mountain but spent much time herding sheep higher.

Why didn't the Iceman have a working bow and arrows? One clue came from the quiver. It was damaged and the cover was missing. Scientists think this may have happened when the two arrows were broken. They also believe the Iceman's bow broke at the same time. A used bowstring, perhaps from the broken bow, was in his backpack.

Top right: *Herders still bring their flocks high in the Alps where the Iceman was found.*
Above: *The Iceman's ax was perfectly preserved by the ice and snow that covered it.*

A VICTIM OF VIOLENCE

Piecing together these clues, Spindler and his team developed a theory about what happened to the Iceman. They believe he was a victim of violence. They think his broken ribs, damaged quiver, and broken bow and arrows all happened at the same time. Then he fled to the mountains where he tried to recover and repair his weapons.

To find out how long before death the violence occurred, Spindler consulted experimental archaeologists. Experimental archaeologists try to do everyday things people did in the past, exactly as they were done in the past. Spindler wanted to know how long it took the Iceman to cut down a tree with a copper ax and then carve the wood into a bow. Experimental archaeologist Harm Paulsen and others cut down trees with crude axes like the Iceman's, then carved bows from the wood, all in less than a day's time.

An experimental archaeologist starts a fire using the same simple tools people used thousands of years ago.

An artist trained in anthropology reconstructs the mummy's face, providing an intriguing view of the Iceman as he would have looked in life (inset).

But the Iceman was in pain. It must have taken him much longer to cut the wood and carve his bow. Without a bow, he was unable to hunt, which is probably why he was starving. Growing weaker from hunger and pain, he set down his ax, bow, and backpack. An early snowstorm came up. The Iceman probably knew how dangerous mountain snowstorms can be. Soon the cold overcame him and he lay down. He died as snow began to cover his body. The Iceman's body never thawed. A glacier covered it and did not melt until 1991.

GETTING THE COMPLETE PICTURE

While X rays and the work of experimental archaeologists can answer many questions, computers can take scientists a step farther. CT scanning uses computerized photography to show the inside of a body. CT is short for "computerized tomography." CT scans give a complete picture of a body without disturbing it from the outside. Scientists have used CT scans to study Egyptian mummies without cutting through the elaborate wrappings. Scans of a mummy from the Inca empire have uncovered a mystery surrounding how a young girl lived and died hundreds of years ago.

Five hundred years ago, much of Nevado Ampato, a volcano in Peru, was free of snow, allowing people to build a site for human sacrifice near the summit.

CHILDREN OF THE INCAS

More than five hundred years ago, the Incas were the largest and most powerful nation in North and South America. They lived in the Andes Mountains of western South America. Roads they constructed are still in use. They built huge, beautiful cities on the mountainsides.

Incas not only lived in the mountains, but also worshiped them as gods. They went to great lengths to build places of worship at the very tops of some of the highest mountains in the world.

Spanish priests wrote in the 1500s that the Incas sacrificed children to their mountain gods. One mountain they mentioned was Nevado Ampato, a volcano in Peru. In 1995, anthropologist Johan Reinhard climbed Ampato and discovered three mummies—two young children and a teenage girl. Their bodies had been frozen for five hundred years on the icy mountaintop.

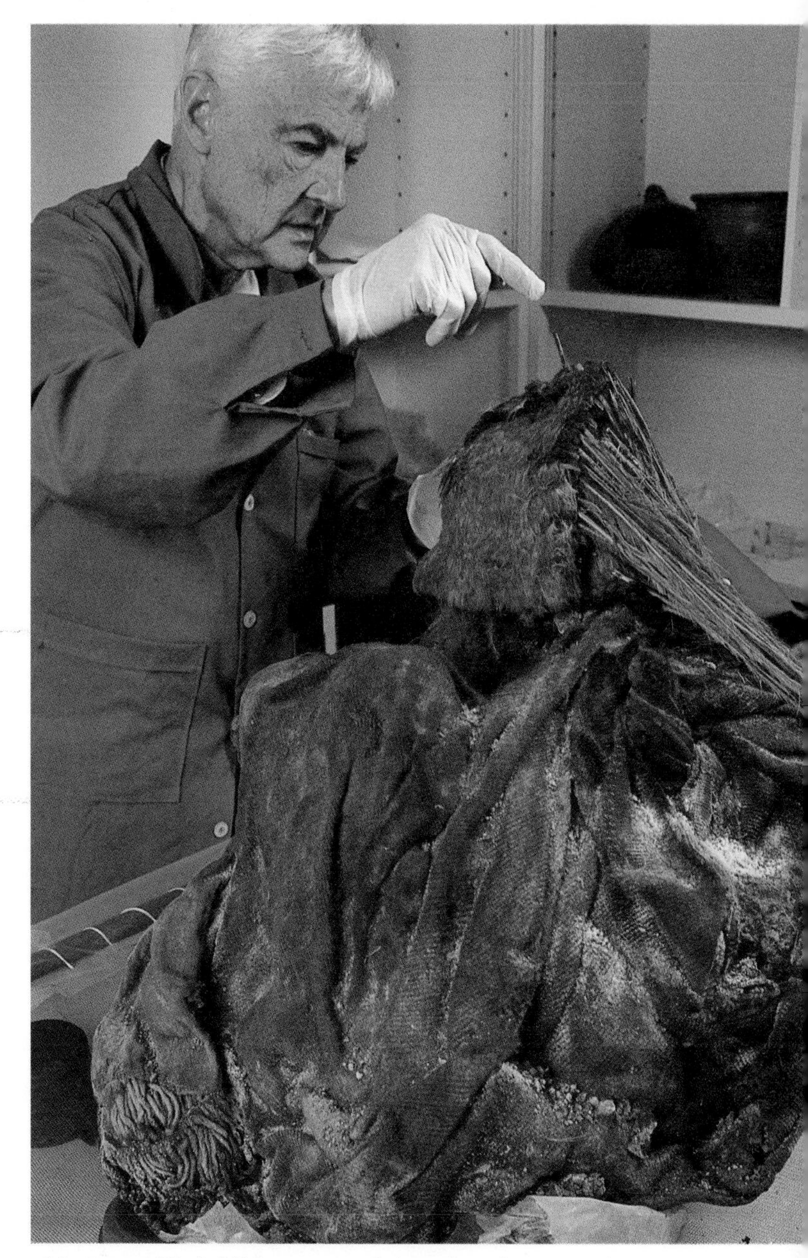

This mummified child was one of three found on Nevado Ampato by anthropologist Johan Reinhard.

The mummies wore beautifully woven clothing. They were buried with jewelry, statues, and decorated dishes. These artifacts all pointed to death by sacrifice, but there was no obvious evidence of violence. Reinhard thought the children probably died peacefully, by suffocation. He figured they were already exhausted from a two-day climb up the mountain. He guessed they were given an alcoholic drink to dull their minds and make them sleepy. Then it would have been easy for an adult to cover their faces until they stopped breathing.

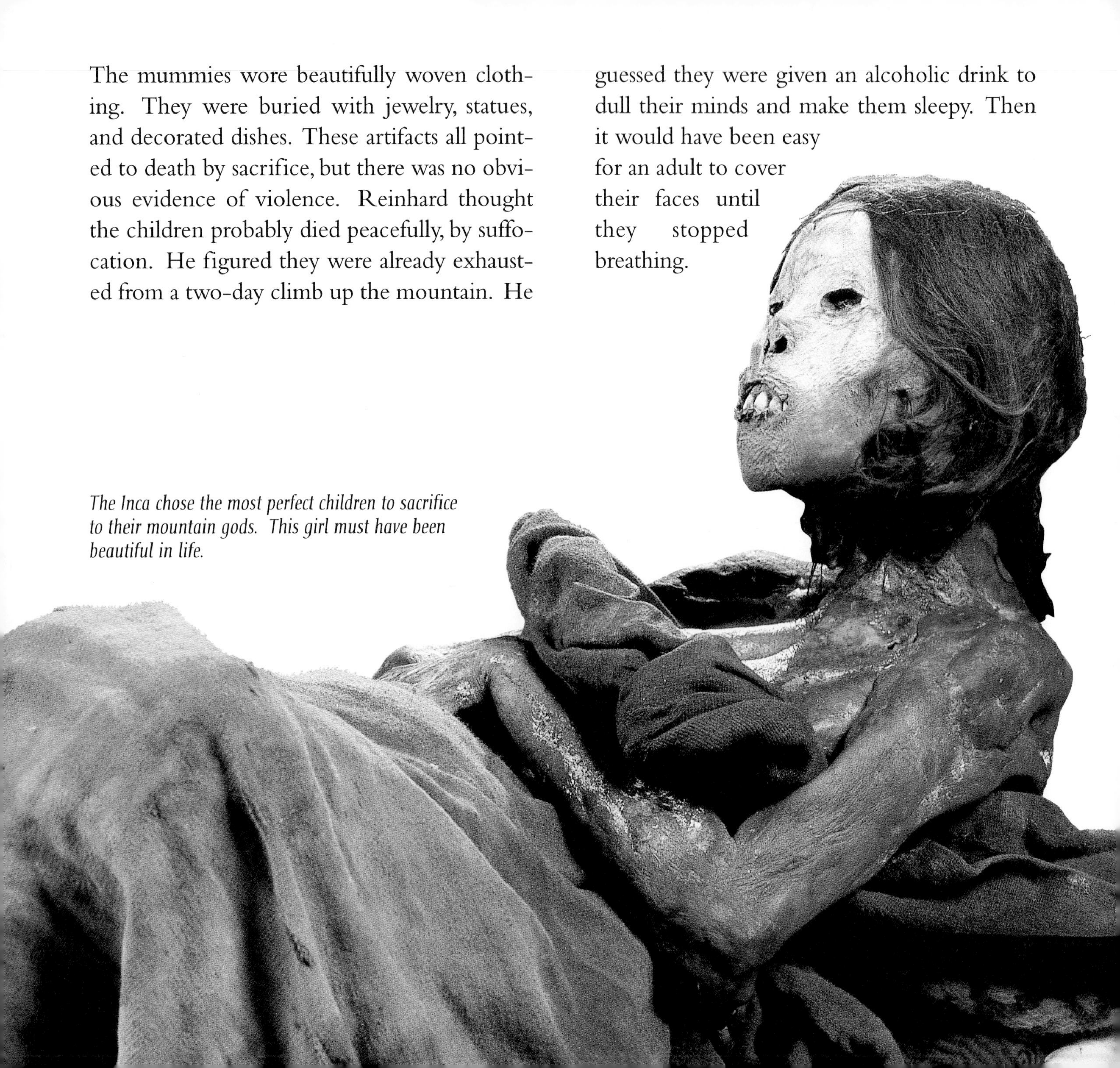

The Inca chose the most perfect children to sacrifice to their mountain gods. This girl must have been beautiful in life.

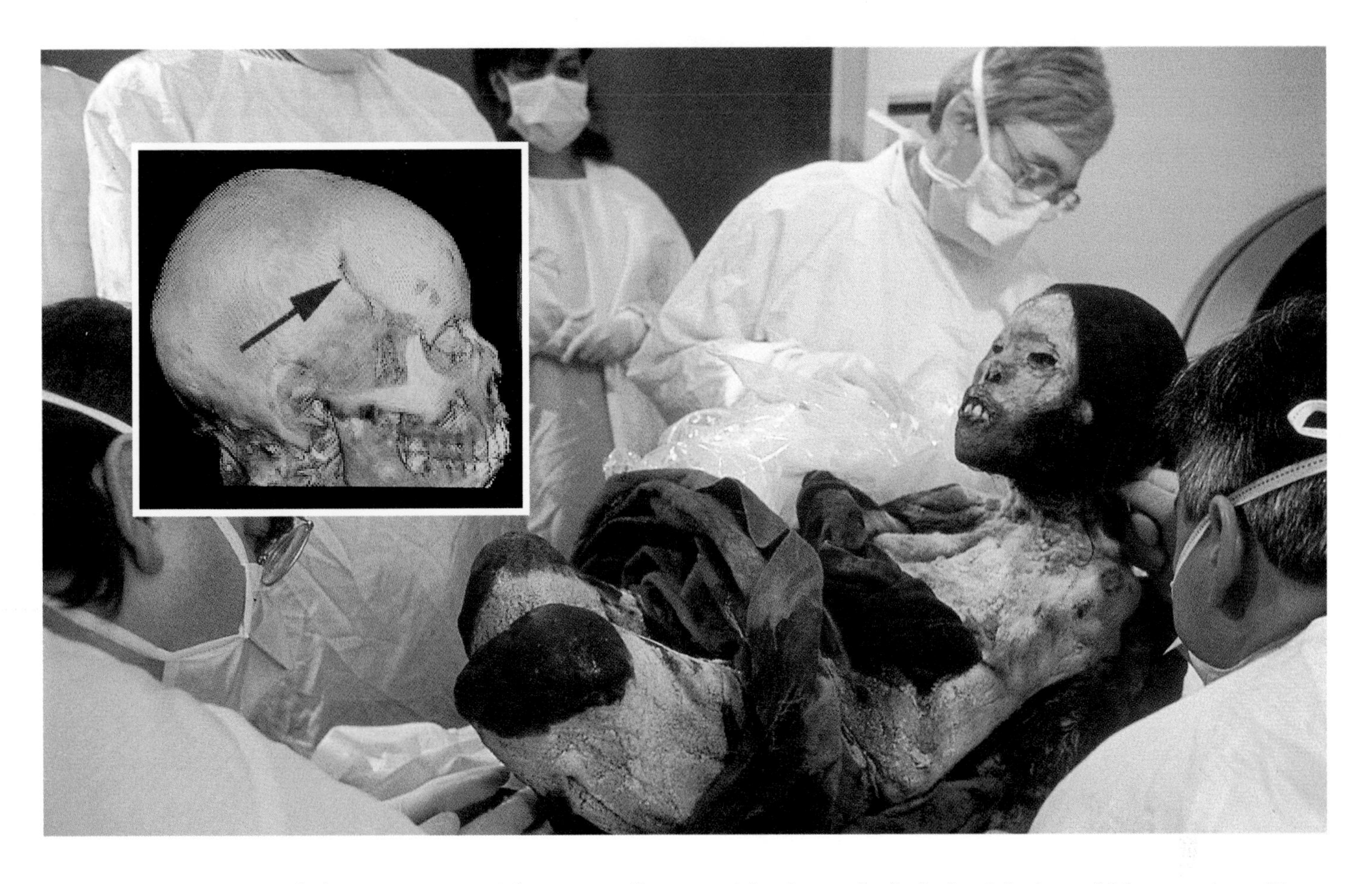

But CT scans of the teenage girl may tell another story. Her skull was broken and her brain was filled with blood from broken blood vessels. Some experts believe she was hit very hard on the head before her death. Other experts believe the skull was fractured later, after the girl died from the cold, still clutching her cloak in her fingers. We may never know what really happened.

Scientists ready the body of the Inca girl for scanning. CT scans (inset) *of the girl's skull reveal a break that may have caused her death five hundred years ago.*

Most people die from natural causes or disease, not human sacrifice. Some South American mummies are helping scientists track one killer. Tuberculosis is a highly contagious disease that usually affects the lungs. It spreads from person to person by coughing and sneezing.

People in Europe, Asia, and Africa suffered from tuberculosis for thousands of years. Scientists once thought tuberculosis did not exist in North and South America until Europeans arrived there. But a thousand-year-old woman from Peru proved otherwise.

While examining the mummy of a woman in Peru, paleopathologist Arthur Aufderheide saw spots on her lungs that looked like tuberculosis. Aufderheide ordered a DNA profile of a sample of the lung tissue. This test looks at the codes carried on DNA molecules within the cells of living things. No one was sure if the test would work on mummified remains. The mummified lung tissue was very fragile. Still, scientists were able to find DNA from a bacterium that causes tuberculosis. This proved that tuberculosis was present in the Americas before Europeans arrived. By testing more mummies for tuberculosis, scientists can track how the disease spread in the past. This knowledge may help them learn how modern-day diseases spread.

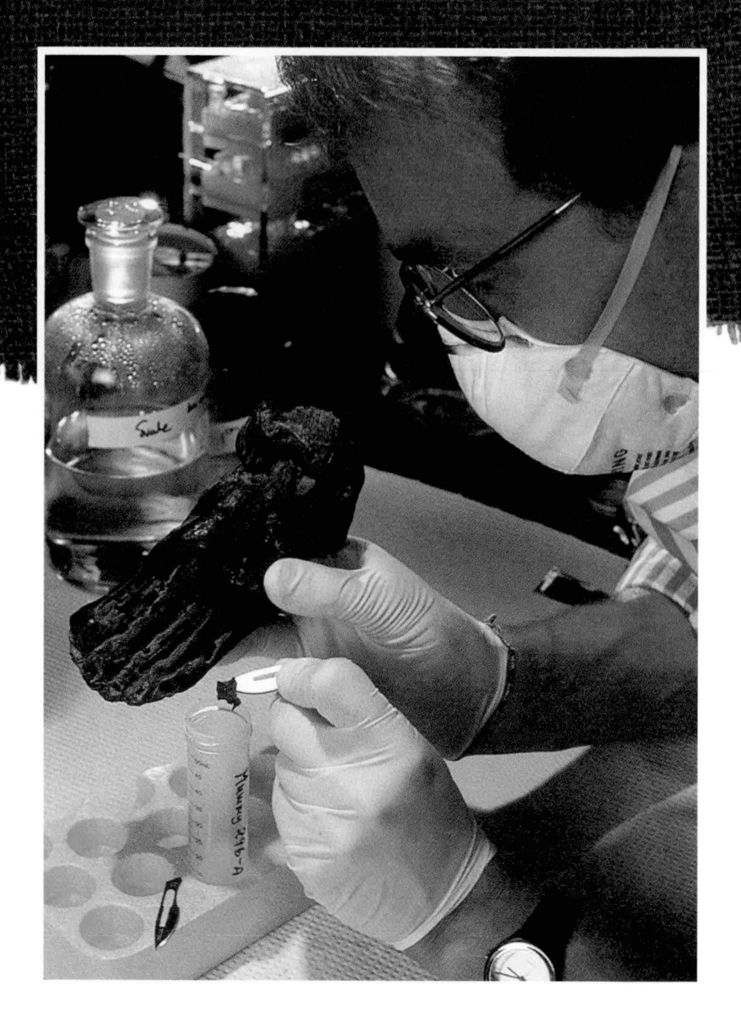

Above: *Mummified lung tissue from Peru helped scientists answer questions about tuberculosis, a highly deadly disease.* Right: *A scientist removes a sample of tissue from an Egyptian mummy's foot for a DNA profile.*

Pathologist Johan Hultin crouches in the bottom of a mass grave in Brevig Mission, Alaska, where victims of the 1918 Spanish flu were buried and mummified in the frozen ground.

ON THE TRAIL OF A KILLER

Scientists hope a frozen mummy who died more than eighty years ago in Brevig Mission, Alaska, may keep us all safe from a killer flu. An especially deadly kind of influenza spread around the world in 1918 and 1919. Influenza, called flu for short, is a contagious disease similar to a bad cold with fever and muscle pains.

Influenza is usually mild and most people fight it off in a few days. But the 1918 flu, called the Spanish flu, turned deadly. It killed nearly a million people in North America and possibly more than forty million worldwide. When it hit Brevig Mission, most of the eighty people who lived there died.

Why did the Spanish flu become deadly in 1918? Could another fast-moving killer flu appear? If it did, could modern medicine save people from dying? Scientists have been trying to answer these questions since 1918.

In 1997, pathologist Johan Hultin went to Brevig Mission in search of tissue samples carrying the Spanish flu virus. The ground there is permanently frozen. Hultin dug up four bodies and found one of them well preserved. From the mummified body, Hultin was able to remove tissue samples containing the Spanish flu virus.

Hultin sent the samples to a research team in Washington, D.C. First the team studied the virus cells for information needed to make a vaccine, just in case the Spanish flu ever comes back. A vaccine is made from dead or weakened germs. The weakened germs are not strong enough to cause harm. They help the body recognize and fight off the disease later when stronger germs of the same kind attack.

The research team continues to study the Spanish flu cells to learn why the disease killed so many in 1918. If scientists can figure out what makes a usually mild disease turn deadly, they may be able to stop future outbreaks.

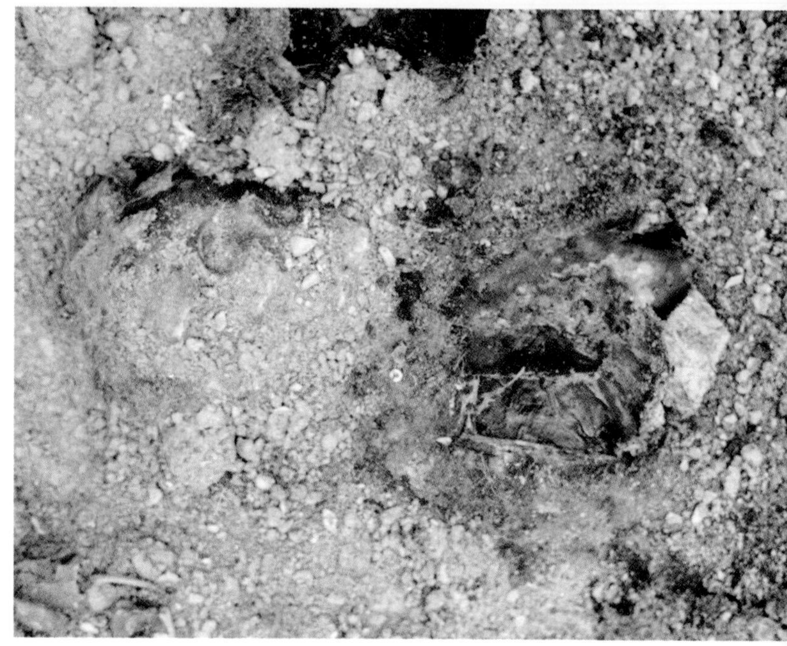

One flu victim, a woman, was well preserved. From her body (top)*, Hultin removed samples of lung tissue* (bottom) *for study.*

This body was buried and naturally mummified in the dry, hot sands near Arica, Chile.

Chapter 5

WHO WERE THEY?

For most people, seeing mummies brings questions to mind. Even after we know when and how people died, we wonder about them. Who were they? Where did they come from? How did they live? Scientists ask these questions too, of mummies and bones and body parts.

When many mummies are buried together over time, scientists can piece together the history of a people even when no written records exist. One of the best places for this type of work is a stretch of desert coastline along the Pacific Ocean in South America. It is the driest place on earth. Bodies buried in the hot sand dry out quickly, often becoming mummies.

People called the Chinchorro buried their dead on these beaches for thousands of years, until about 1500 B.C. Scientists named the people after Chinchorro Beach in Arica, Chile, where some of their dead were found. No one knows what the Chinchorro called themselves. They left no written records. But they left thousands of mummies to tell their story.

This young boy was mummified and his face covered with a paste mask according to the traditions of the Chinchorro, who lived in Chile thousands of years ago.

STORIES STORED INSIDE

The Chinchorro were one of the earliest peoples to practice embalming. Preserving the dead must have been very important to them. They took great pains to embalm bodies. They used an elaborate process that began with removing the skin and muscles.

The skeleton was taken apart and cleaned. Then it was put back together by tying it onto a wooden framework. Next, embalmers covered everything with a body cast made of mud or paste, shaping the face into a mask. Finally the whole thing was painted.

The goal of Chinchorro embalming seems to have been to create a statue out of the dead person. Scientists think the Chinchorro did not bury the bodies right away. Some of the mummies were repainted before burial.

Researchers think they may have been kept in the family home or put on display before being buried.

The Chinchorro bodies have many stories to tell. By examining their bones and intestines, scientists learned the Chinchorro got most of their food from the sea. Sea lion meat, fish, shellfish, and seaweed provided good nutrition.

The bodies of Chinchorro men and women showed some differences. Many of the men had growths in their ears caused by spending much time in cold water. This shows that the men probably did most of the fishing and diving for shellfish and seaweed. Many men, but none of the women, had small breaks in bones of their lower backs. These probably happened from falling on slippery rocks along the shore.

Chinchorro women suffered from a different back problem. Their bones were not healthy, probably because they did not have enough calcium in their diet during pregnancy and nursing.

Some researchers think Chinchorro beliefs about caring for the dead may have been responsible for another health problem. Nearly half the Chinchorro mummies studied had serious infections on their legs. Scientists believe these infections could have been caused by constant contact with dead bodies.

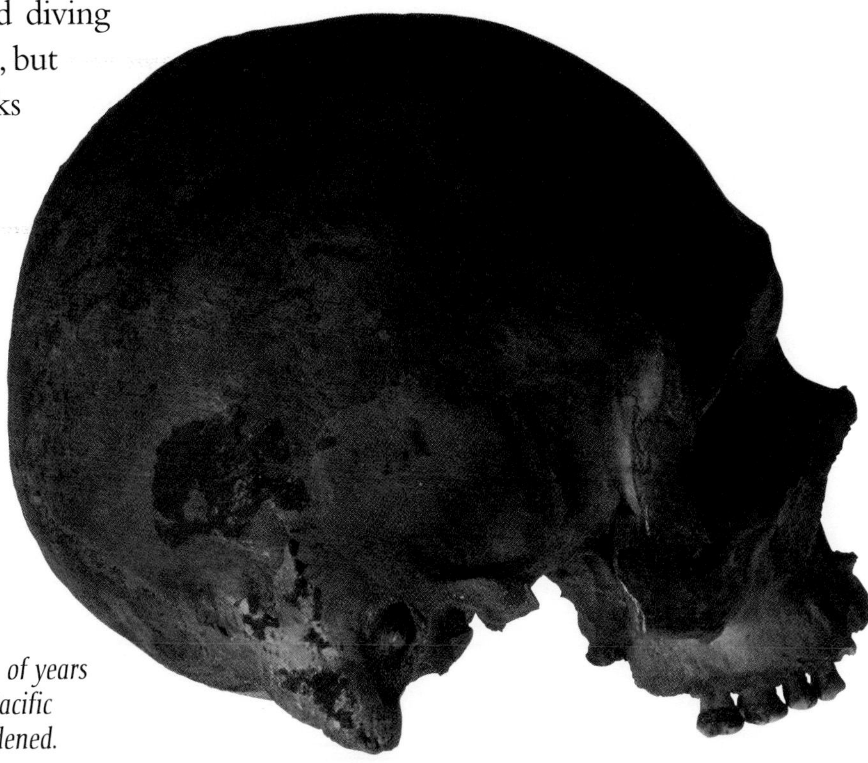

The skull of a Chinchorro man shows the effects of years of diving for shellfish in the cold waters of the Pacific Ocean. The bone around the ear canal has hardened.

AN OASIS FULL OF MUMMIES

The ways in which people care for the dead change over time, even in a place like Egypt with its world-famous mummies and tombs. One day in 1996, an Egyptian man was riding his donkey to work at a temple in the Bahariya Oasis in central Egypt. As the man's donkey walked along the path, its foot fell into a hole. The man looked into the hole and saw gold-covered mummies lying side by side. Until that day, no one knew they were there.

Egyptian scientists rushed to Bahariya Oasis to investigate. After months of work, they located about 150 underground tombs, containing thousands of mummies. More tombs may yet be discovered.

A stumbling donkey helped uncover tombs filled with mummies at the Bahariya Oasis in central Egypt. Settlements there date back 2,300 years. Archaeologists believe that people living at the Bahariya Oasis in ancient times became wealthy growing grapes for making wine.

A SPECIAL KIND OF MUMMY

Who were the people buried in these tombs? The Bahariya Oasis mummies are different from most other Egyptian mummies. They are people who lived during the time when Greece and Rome controlled Egypt (from 332 B.C. to about A.D. 350). Most Egyptian mummies are older, dating from the time when Egyptians ruled their own land.

When Greece and Rome conquered Egypt, they brought European beliefs and traditions. The people of the Bahariya Oasis mixed these foreign beliefs with their ancient Egyptian traditions. Burial masks on the Bahariya Oasis mummies show Greek-style portraits with European hairdos. Paintings of Greek, Roman, and Egyptian gods decorate the mummy wrappings. Many mummies were not buried in traditional Egyptian coffins but were simply wrapped and placed in tombs.

These mummies are important to scientists for another reason. At the Bahariya Oasis, people lived and buried their dead in the same place for more than six hundred years. Whole families are buried together, sometimes for several generations. The Bahariya Oasis mummies can help scientists track how peoples' lives changed over the centuries. Their story will unfold for years to come as scientists continue to study them.

Further study of decorative coffins, some covered with gold, will provide clues about how Greek and Roman traditions mixed with traditional Egyptian beliefs in the years when Greece and Rome ruled Egypt.

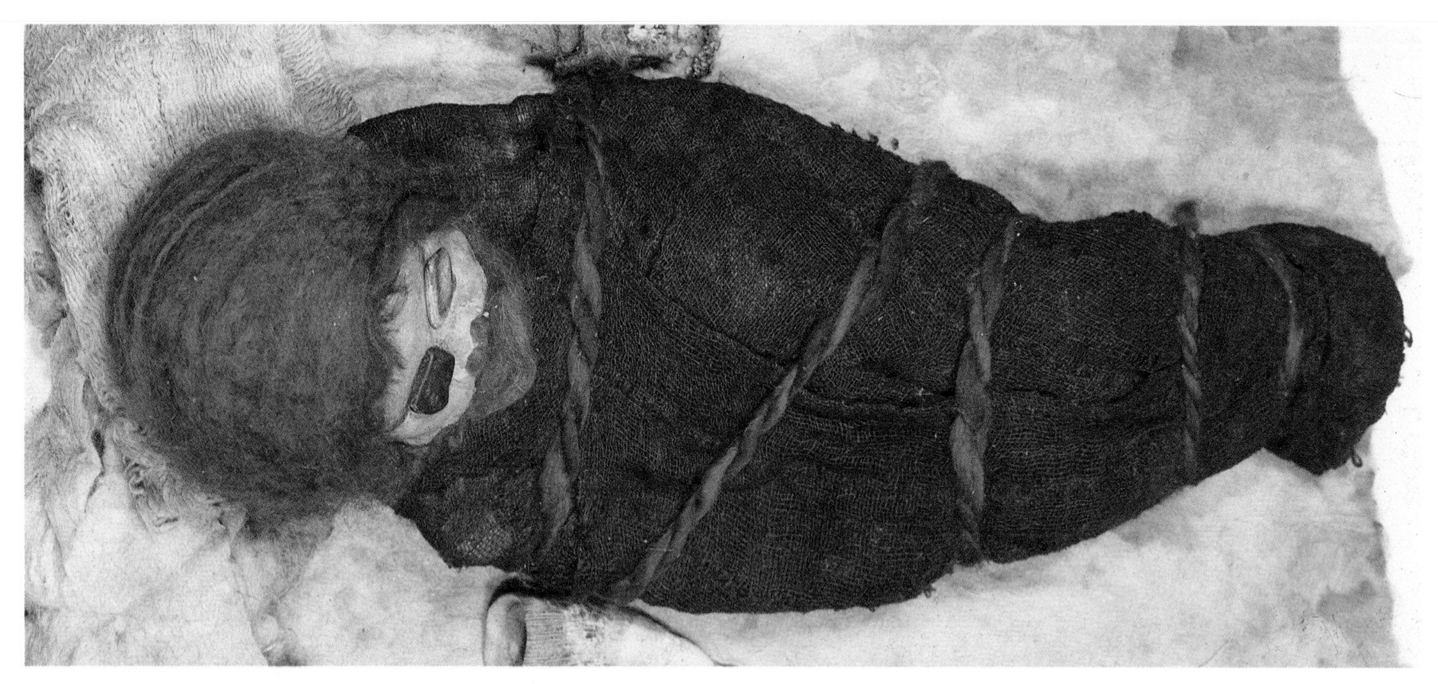

Wisps of light-colored hair escape from the woolen headwrap worn by this mummified infant from Xinjiang, China. Soft stones cover the baby's eyes.

EUROPEANS IN ANCIENT CHINA

Human remains can also help scientists piece together where people came from in the ancient past. Mummies found in the province of Xinjiang in northwestern China surprised many scientists. The mummies are three to four thousand years old, preserved by the desert climate in which they were buried.

What is surprising about these mummies is that they have light skin and European-looking features. Many have light-colored hair. People with these traits are called Caucasian. More than one hundred Caucasian bodies have been discovered in China. All were found along China's Silk Road. The Silk Road carried traders from the West into China to buy silk, tea, and other goods.

Historians knew that Caucasian people traveled to China in the ancient past. But until recently most scientists did not think they lived in China. The large number of Caucasian mummies in Xinjiang, home to the Uygur people, proved that idea wrong.

Modern-day residents of Xinjiang, China, were so taken by the beauty of this Caucasian mummy (above) *that they wrote a song in her honor* (right).

The Uygur people of modern Xinjiang look more Caucasian than Chinese. They speak their own language and have their own form of writing. The Chinese government wants the Uygur to adopt Chinese ways, but they have resisted. The discovery of Caucasian mummies has only added to the tension.

Human remains can link modern-day people with ancient groups. Some groups, including the Uygur of Xinjiang, appreciate knowing more about their ancestors. But discoveries of human remains can sometimes bring more questions than answers. They add fuel to the debate about whether it is right to dig up the dead and study their bones.

In the late 1800s, adventurers such as Earl Morris (above, left) *combed the American Southwest looking for ancient remains, pottery, tools, and baskets. Modern-day archaeologists in Asia unearthed these skulls* (opposite) *for study.*

Chapter 6

WHAT TO DO WITH MUMMIES AND BONES

People long ago probably never imagined that their bodies might be uncovered after burial. They probably never thought that scientists would study their tissue under a microscope, or that grave robbers might disturb their bones. But dead bodies and body parts have been handled—and mishandled—over the centuries. How to treat human remains continues to be an important question all over the world.

In North America, it is illegal for people to keep human remains they find. Often remains are turned over to the police, to doctors, or to the government. Experts try to identify the body and find living relatives whenever possible. Those relatives are usually allowed to rebury the body or bones as long as they are not needed to solve a crime.

Identifying Human Remains

Twenty-five years after the end of the Vietnam War, the remains of U.S. soldiers are still being returned. When the Vietnamese government turns a body or bones over to the Americans, often no one knows who it is. The remains are placed in a coffin and draped with an American flag. They are then flown to the U.S. Army Central Identification Laboratory in Hawaii.

When the plane lands in Hawaii, it is met by an honor guard of soldiers from every branch of the military in dress uniforms. The reason for this is that no one knows in which branch the dead person served. The honor guard marches into the airplane and carries the coffin to the laboratory.

Inside the laboratory, scientists study the remains. No one may enter the room without permission, and all who enter must remove their hats in honor of the dead. All remains are covered with white sheets when they are not being examined. In the evening, all sheets are neatly folded once again to cover every set of remains, even the smallest pile of bones.

When a set of remains is identified, it is once again placed in a coffin and covered with an American flag. Another honor guard, this time from the branch of the military in which the dead person served, carries the coffin to an airplane. It is then flown to the soldier's family.

The body of an American serviceman, First Lieutenant Michael Blassie, was buried in 1998. Killed during the Vietnam War in 1972, his remains were positively identified using DNA testing.

LEAVING BONES ALONE

When no living relatives are found, it's harder to know what to do with old bones. Should they be put on display? Should scientists be able to study them? A growing number of people believe scientists should leave dead bodies alone.

Some Native Americans have gone to court to force scientists to hand over skeletons. They have then reburied the remains with religious ceremonies.

Called the Indian Burial Pit by its owners, this Native American burial place (left) *near Salina, Kansas, was operated as a tourist attraction beginning in the 1930s. Pawnee and other Indians successfully fought for the right to close the attraction and rebury their ancestors* (above) *in 1990.*

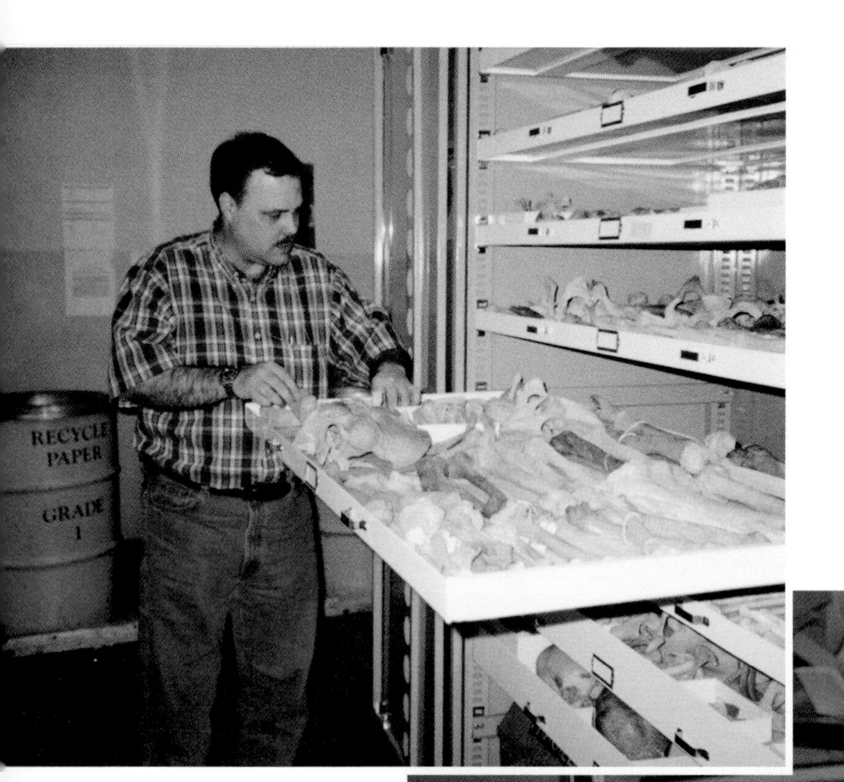

In 1990, the U.S. Congress passed the Native American Graves Protection and Repatriation Act. This act gives Native Americans control over all native remains buried on government lands or held in collections owned or funded by the government. The same act makes it illegal for anyone to sell native dead bodies. Many native skeletons and mummies are still stored in schools and private collections across the country, but Native American groups are working to change this.

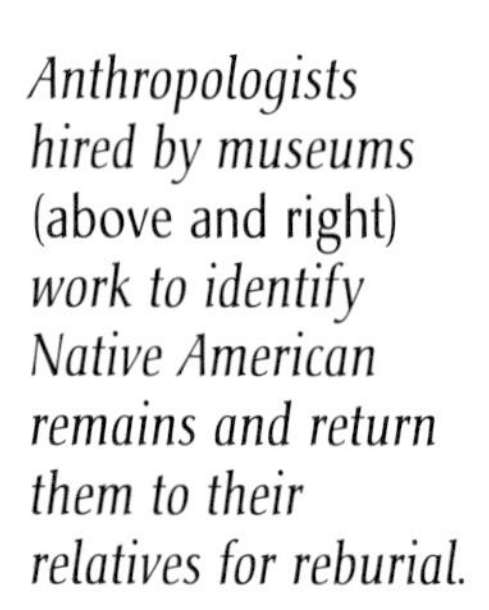

Anthropologists hired by museums (above and right) *work to identify Native American remains and return them to their relatives for reburial.*

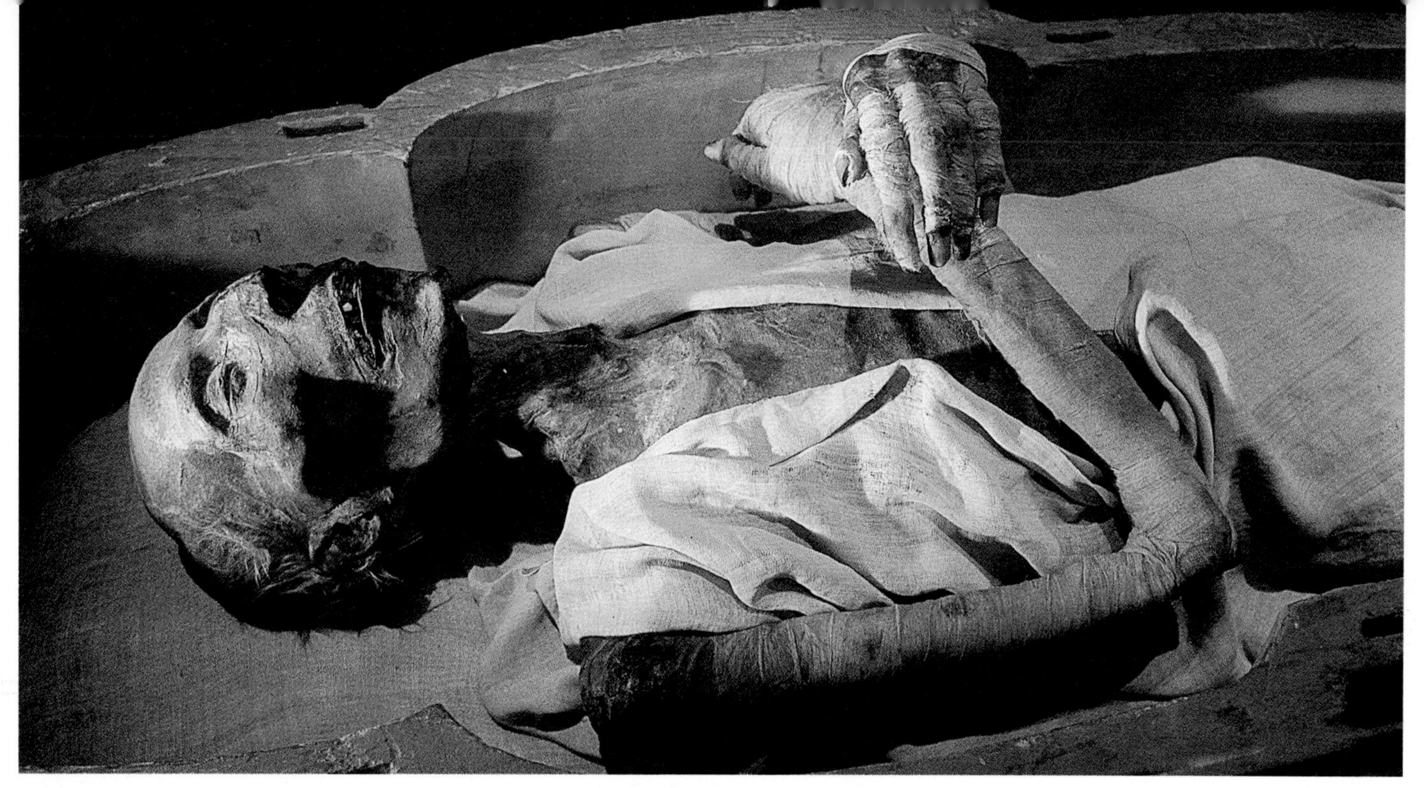

King Ramses II rests in the Royal Mummies Room at the Egyptian Museum in Cairo in a case designed to protect his remains from decay and damage.

A NEW HOME FOR EGYPT'S KINGS

People in other parts of the world are also trying to preserve the dignity of human remains. Anwar Sadat, former president of Egypt, was saddened by the way the ancient kings of Egypt were displayed at the Egyptian Museum in Cairo, Egypt. The museum was old and rundown. Some of the mummies were not well cared for. In 1979, Sadat ordered the royal mummy display shut down. He did not think it was worthy of the mummies' noble ranks.

The museum spent many years giving the royal mummies a new home called the Royal Mummies Room. This room has special cases that protect the mummies from decay and damage. Visitors are not allowed to talk when they tour the room, in honor of the dead. The Egyptian government hopes their new mummy room will encourage other museums to show more respect for dead bodies on display.

MUMMIES AND BONES FOR SALE

Over the years, people have tried to profit from human bodies and burial grounds. Grave robbers have been at work since the days of ancient Egypt. In North and South America, people continue to dig up Native American graves because they know collectors will pay high prices for the artifacts. Many times the bones are simply left scattered on the ground.

Sometimes people turn the dead into sideshow attractions. A store in Seattle, Washington, has human mummies on display for customers to look at while they shop. The mummies are more than one hundred years old. One was found shot to death in the Arizona desert and was naturally mummified. Another was from Central America. They ended up as store props because no one knew who they were and no one thought to bury them.

Sylvester, as his owners call him, greets customers at Ye Olde Curiosity Shop in Seattle, Washington.

Elmer McCurdy was put on display for sixty-five years before he was finally buried. McCurdy was a train robber who was shot in Oklahoma in 1911. His body was taken to the local funeral parlor. When the funeral director learned that McCurdy had no family to pay for embalming, he decided to let McCurdy pay for it himself. The funeral director embalmed McCurdy with extra-strong materials. Then he charged people money to see the outlaw.

One day a visitor told the funeral director that McCurdy was his brother and he wanted to bury him. The funeral director gave the man the body, but it was not buried. The man was not McCurdy's brother, but a carnival operator. McCurdy spent the next fifty years or more traveling in carnival sideshows.

In 1976, the crew of *The Six-Million Dollar Man* television show went to an amusement park to film a scene. The plot involved a chase through a house of horrors. When a crew member picked up what he thought was a fake dead man, an arm fell off. A human bone was clearly seen, and the police were called. When the body was identified as McCurdy's, it was finally claimed and sent to Oklahoma to be buried, sixty-five years late.

Elmer McCurdy's burial was postponed by sixty-five years, as people profited from the display of his mummified body.

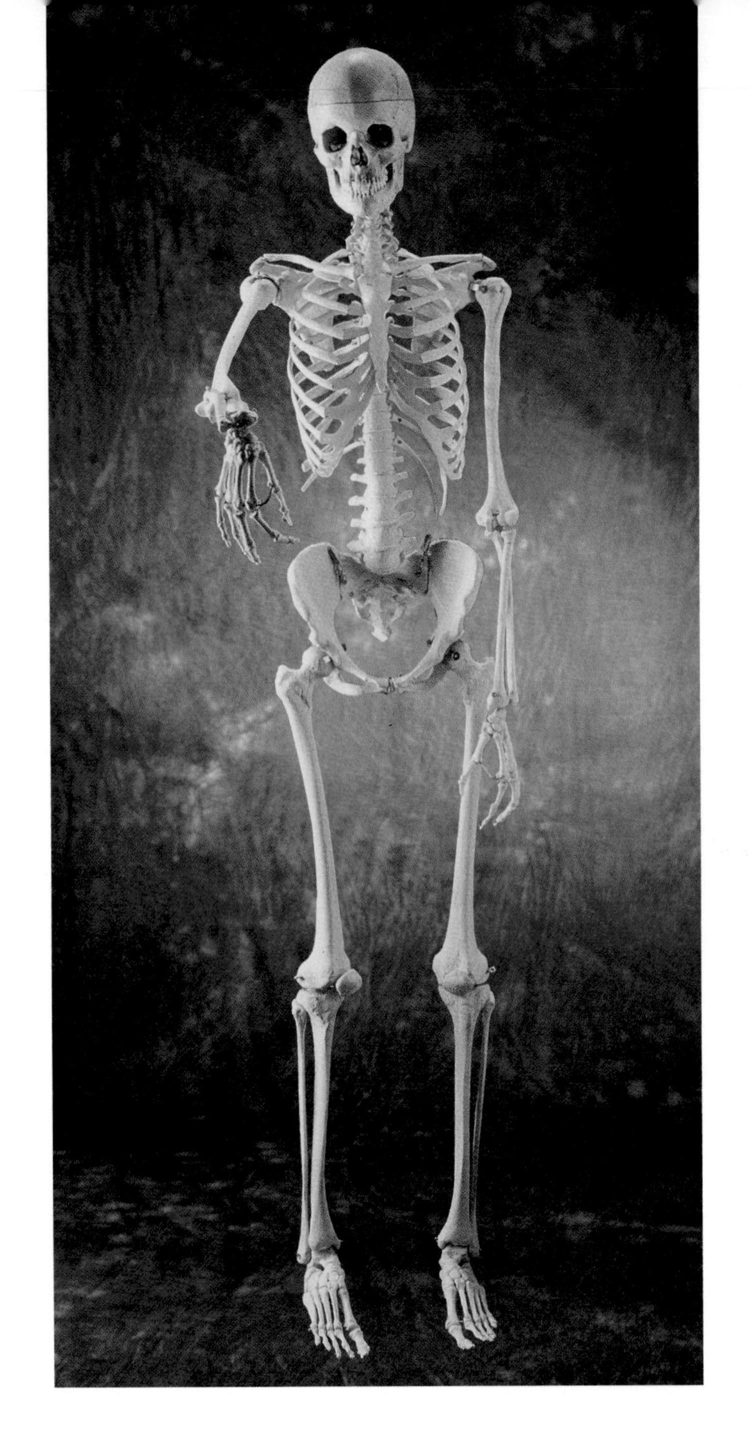

BODIES AND PARTS FOR SALE

For several hundred years, well-preserved bodies and body parts have been used in medical schools. The body parts give students a firsthand look inside the human body. In times gone by, teachers in medical schools earned money by selling tickets to their classes. They always wanted to have the most eye-catching dead bodies. The more students who took their classes, the more money they made.

Modern medical schools use dead bodies just for study, not for making money. Some of these bodies are donated by people before death. Others are bodies of people who had no relatives to claim them for burial. Many classrooms have real skeletons on display to teach about the human body. But the best specimens are those with soft tissues.

Many people donate their bodies to science so that, after death, their organs can help those awaiting transplants or their skeletons can help students learning about human anatomy.

One way of preserving soft tissues is called plastination. It makes modern mummies that help doctors learn surgery and other skills. Plastination was developed in Germany about twenty years ago. Tissues are freeze-dried to remove all water. Then the water is replaced with plastic. The process takes several months. The result is a very lifelike specimen that keeps the color and shape of living tissue. Plastination is mostly performed on parts of bodies, although whole bodies have also been treated in this way. It is accepted worldwide as the best way to preserve human body tissue for teaching medical students.

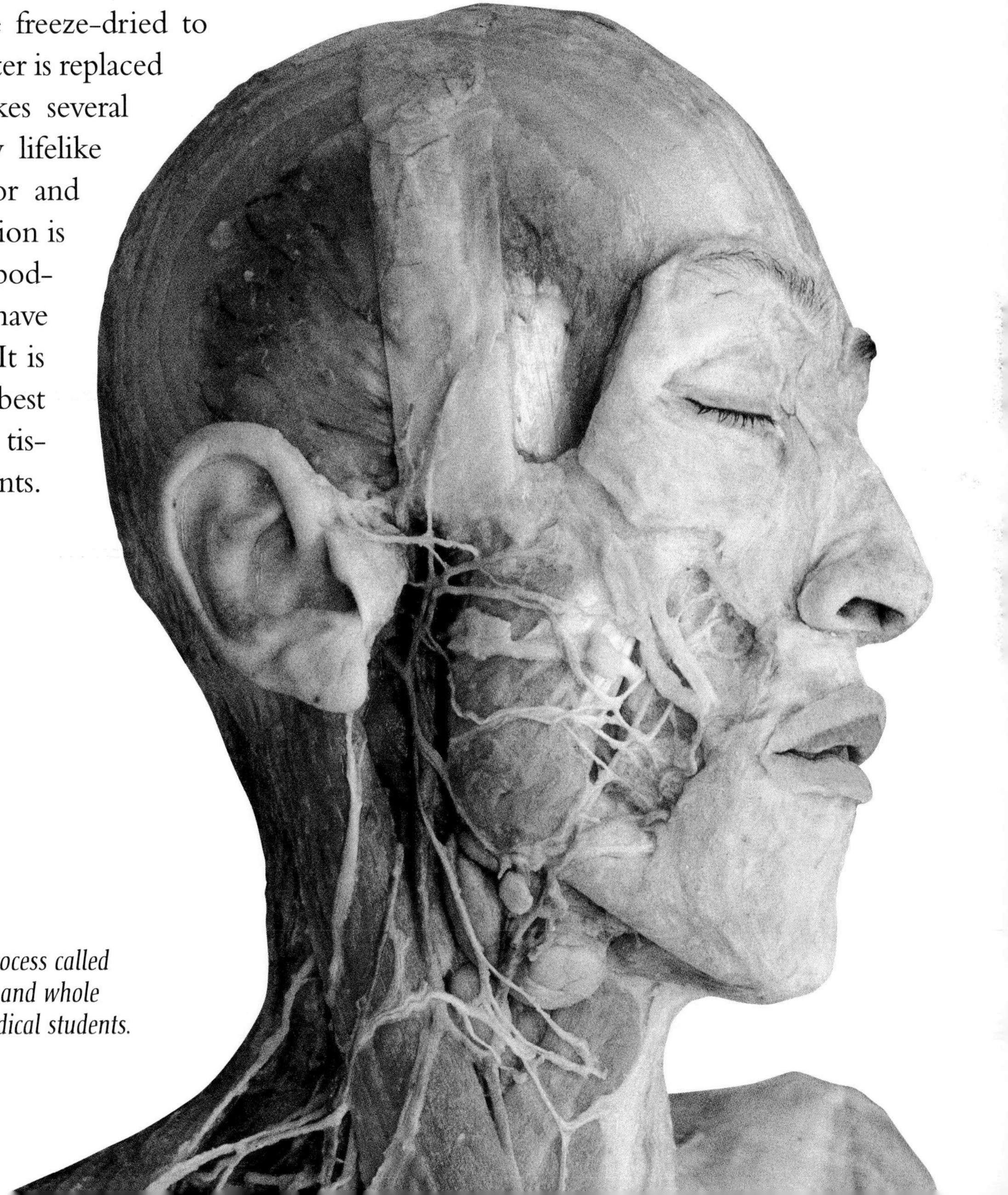

This human head was preserved by a process called plastination. Plastinated organs, limbs, and whole bodies provide lifelike specimens for medical students.

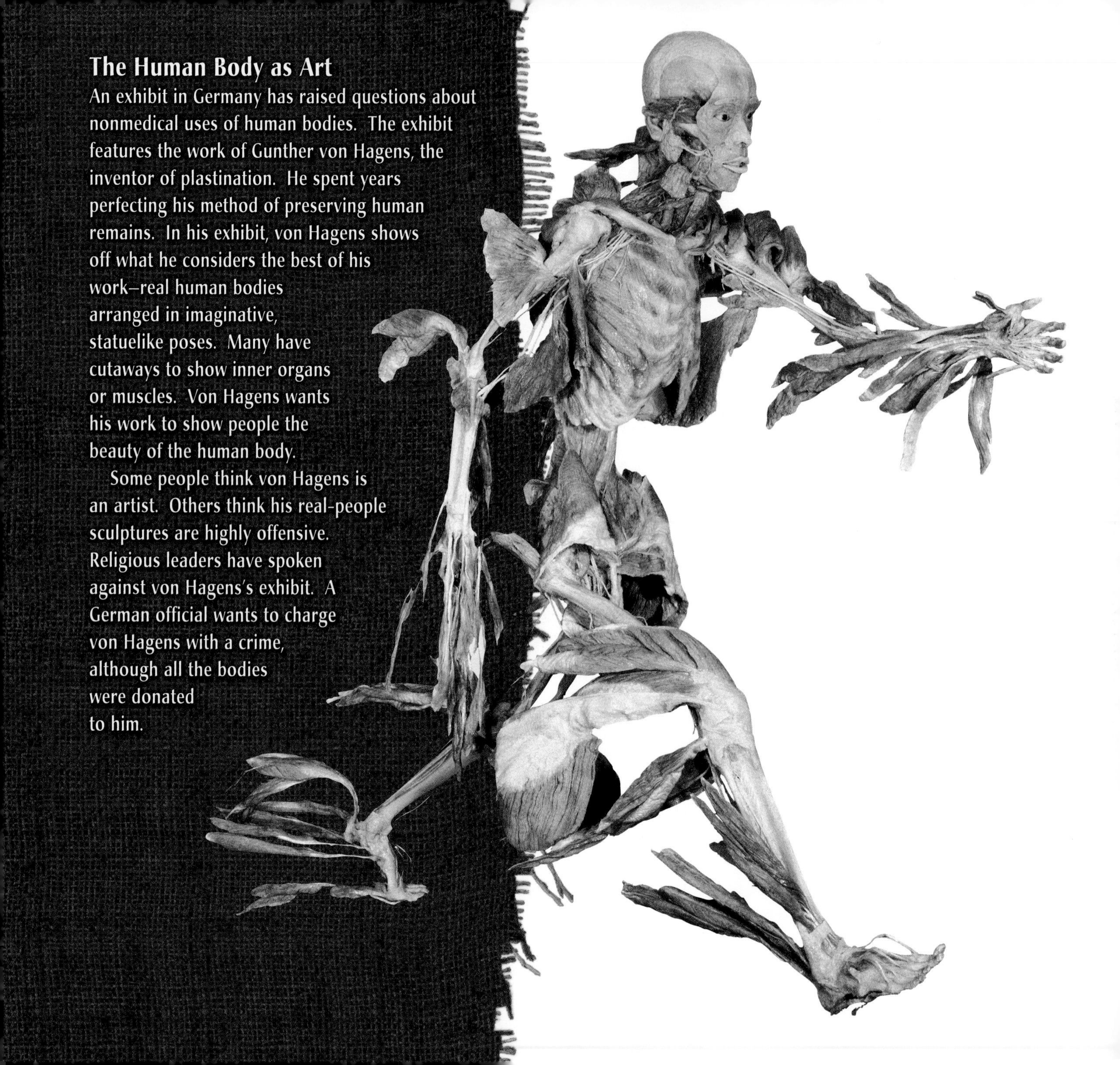

The Human Body as Art

An exhibit in Germany has raised questions about nonmedical uses of human bodies. The exhibit features the work of Gunther von Hagens, the inventor of plastination. He spent years perfecting his method of preserving human remains. In his exhibit, von Hagens shows off what he considers the best of his work–real human bodies arranged in imaginative, statuelike poses. Many have cutaways to show inner organs or muscles. Von Hagens wants his work to show people the beauty of the human body.

Some people think von Hagens is an artist. Others think his real-people sculptures are highly offensive. Religious leaders have spoken against von Hagens's exhibit. A German official wants to charge von Hagens with a crime, although all the bodies were donated to him.

PUTTING THE DEAD TO REST

In recent years, there has been great interest in studying dead bodies. New technology allows scientists to learn much more from human remains than they could in the past. More efforts are being made than ever before to study mummies, bones, and body parts. This bothers people who believe respect for the dead is more important than what can be learned by digging up remains.

But in some cases, scientists rescue ancient bodies from a worse fate, grave robbing. This is a serious problem, even in the most out-of-the-way places. Grave robbers often destroy bodies and bones or leave them scattered out in the open.

If scientists had not dug up the Pazyryk lady, would she still be resting peacefully in her mountain grave? Or would robbers have found her gold and treasures by now, leaving her body to decay in the sun?

No one can make certain that every dead body will rest quietly in the earth. But scientists and religious and cultural leaders are beginning to work together to make sure all human remains are treated with the respect their families wanted them to have.

This person died thousands of years ago in Peru but will no longer enjoy a quiet rest. The mummy and clothes will be preserved for study, allowing scientists to learn more about our human past.

GLOSSARY

archaeologist: a scientist who investigates the past by studying artifacts, buildings, ancient writing, and other objects

autopsy: an examination performed on a dead person, usually to find the cause of death

bacteria: microscopic living things that exist almost everywhere. Many bacteria are useful, but some cause disease.

cryonics: the practice of freezing the body of a person who dies, in hopes of bringing the person back to life at a future time

CT scan: sometimes called CAT scan, short for computerized axial tomography. This special kind of X ray uses computerized photography to show the inside of a body.

DNA: short for deoxyribonucleic acid, the molecule carrying the information or special codes that give each living thing its unique characteristics

DNA profile: a laboratory test that analyzes the codes carried on DNA molecules

embalming: treating a dead body in order to preserve it from decay

experimental archaeologist: a person trained and skilled in trying to duplicate everyday things people did in the past, exactly as they were done in the past

forensic anthropologist: a scientist who studies human remains for the purpose of solving crimes or settling disputes in court

mummification: the process of turning a dead body into a mummy. Mummification occurs naturally, as when a body is quickly dried or frozen, or by embalming.

mummy: a body in which the soft tissues did not decay after death

paleopathologist: a scientist who studies ancient human remains, especially preserved soft tissues

physical anthropologist: a scientist who studies human remains for the purpose of learning about human history

plastination: a method of preserving body tissue by replacing the water in it with plastic

radiocarbon dating: estimating the age of old material by measuring how much of a certain type of carbon atom it contains

rehydration: the process of putting water back into tissues that once were moist but have dried out

remains: a dead body or parts of something that was once alive

soft tissue: skin, muscles, and organs

vaccine: a substance containing dead, weakened, or living organisms that can be injected or taken orally. The vaccine causes a person to produce antibodies that protect against the disease caused by the organisms.

X ray: a photograph made by a special camera that uses invisible, high-energy beams of light that can pass through solid objects

When people bury their loved ones, they rarely imagine that others may uncover the remains years later. Here archaeologists uncover mummies in an Egyptian tomb.

SELECTED BIBLIOGRAPHY

Allen, Thomas B. "The Silk Road's Lost World." *National Geographic* (March 1996): 44-51.

Arriaza, Bernardo. "Chile's Chinchorro Mummies." *National Geographic* (March 1995): 68-89.

Aufderheide, Arthur C., and Conrado Rodrìguez-Martin. *The Cambridge Encyclopedia of Human Paleopathology.* Cambridge, England: Cambridge University Press, 1998.

Brier, Bob. *The Encyclopedia of Mummies.* New York: Checkmark Books, 1998.

Christensen, D. "Pre-Columbian Mummies Lay TB Debate to Rest." *Science News* (March 19, 1994):181.

Franklin-Barbajosa, Cassandra. "The New Face of Identity." *National Geographic* (May 1992): 112-124.

Hadingham, Evan. "The Mummies of Xinjiang." *Discover* (April 1994): 68-77.

Hawass, Zahi. "Oasis of the Dead." *Archaeology* (September/October 1999): 38-43.

Larson, Erik. "The Flu Hunters." *Time* (February 23, 1998): 53-64.

Maples, William R., and Michael Browning. *Dead Men Do Tell Tales.* New York: Doubleday, 1994.

Polosmak, Natalya. "A Mummy Unearthed from the Pastures of Heaven." *National Geographic* (October 1994): 80-103.

Reinhard, Johan. "Peru's Ice Maidens." *National Geographic* (June 1996): 62-81.

Reinhard, Johan. "Sacred Peaks of the Andes." *National Geographic* (March 1992): 84-111.

Reinhard, Johan. "Sharp Eyes of Science Probe the Mummies of Peru." *National Geographic* (January 1997): 36-43.

Roberts, David. "The Iceman." *National Geographic* (June 1993): 36-67.

Spindler, Konrad, et al. *Human Mummies.* New York: Springer-Verlag Wien, 1996.

"Tales from the Crypt." *Time* (April 18, 1994): 67.

Toufexis, Anastasia. "The Mummy's Tale." *Time* (March 28, 1994): 53.

Turner, R. C., and R. G. Scaife. *Bog Bodies: New Discoveries and New Perspectives.* London: British Museum Press, 1995.

Webster, Donovan. "Valley of the Mummies." *National Geographic* (October 1999): 76-87.

Weeks, Kent R. "Valley of the Kings." *National Geographic* (September 1998): 2-33.

RESOURCES ON MUMMIES

For Further Reading

Deem, James M. *Bodies from the Bog.* Boston: Houghton Mifflin Company, 1998. Deem explores the lives and deaths of people whose bodies have been preserved for hundreds of years in peat bogs throughout Europe.

Deem, James M. Illustrated by True Kelley. *How to Make a Mummy Talk.* Boston: Houghton Mifflin Company, 1995. Deem explores all kinds of myths surrounding mummies.

Echo-Hawk, Roger C. and Walter R. Echo-Hawk. *Battlefields and Burial Grounds: The Indian Struggle to Protect Ancestral Graves in the United States.* Minneapolis, MN: Lerner Publications Company, 1994. The authors look at the treatment of Native American remains and efforts to return remains to living relatives.

Getz, David. *Frozen Girl.* New York: Henry Holt and Company, 1998. In this chapter book, Getz uses interviews with scientists to tell the story of the young Inca girl whose mummified body was found in Peru by anthropologist Johan Reinhard.

Jackson, Donna M. *The Bone Detectives: How Forensic Anthropologists Solve Crimes and Uncover Mysteries of the Dead.* Boston: Little, Brown and Company, 1995. Illustrated with many photographs, this book tells the story of scientists who study bones, hair, teeth, and other human remains to find missing persons and solve crimes.

Quinlan, Susan E. *The Case of the Mummified Pigs and Other Mysteries in Nature.* Honesdale, PA: Boyds Mills Press, 1995. In the title essay in this collection, Quinlan explains how, by experimenting with dead piglets, one scientist helped determine why most bodies decompose, but others become mummies.

Reinhard, Johan. *Discovering the Inca Ice Maiden: My Adventures on Ampato.* Washington, DC: National Geographic Society, 1998. In words and photographs, Dr. Reinhard, an anthropologist, recounts his discovery of the mummified body of a young girl from the time of the Incas.

Wilcox, Charlotte. *Mummies & Their Mysteries.* Minneapolis, MN: Carolrhoda Books, Inc., 1993. Using many photographs to illustrate her points, Wilcox outlines the different kinds of mummies found around the world and explains how they are made or how they occur naturally.

Websites

For a wealth of information on mummies, search for the word mummies at
http://www.pbs.org/wgbh/nova/search.html

For information on cryonic storage, see
http://www.cryonics.org

For information on bog bodies, see
http://uts.cc.utexas.edu/~dente/bogbodies.htm

For information on Canada's Iceman from the 1450s, see
http://www.archaeology.org/online/news/iceman

For an interactive journey with anthropologist Johan Reinhard, see
http://www.nationalgeographic.com/mummy/index.html

For information on efforts to return Native American remains to living relatives, see
http://www.nmnh.si.edu/anthro/repatriation/

For a review of Gunther von Hagens's plastinated human sculptures, see
http://www.shul.org/corpse.htm

INDEX

References to captions appear in italics.

ACKNOWLEDGEMENTS

The photographs in this book are reproduced through the courtesy of: The National Museum of Denmark, pp. 1, 24; © Stephen Alvarez, pp. 2, 32, 33, 34; © Eric Brissaud/Liaison Agency, pp. 5, 13; Laura Westlund, p. 6; © Charles O'Rear/Corbis, pp. 7, 8, 9; © Nicole Thompson, p. 10; © Corbis/Bettmann-UPI, p. 11; © Kenneth Garrett, pp. 12, 15, 17, 27 (top), 28 (bottom), 29 (both), 30, 31 (both), 42, 43, 51, 59, 64; Cryonics Institute, p. 14; © Marc Deville/Liaison Agency, pp. 16, 57; © National Museum of Ireland, p. 18; Sam Vastro, Radiocarbon Laboratory, University of Texas at Austin, p. 19; Cheshire County Constabulary, p. 20; The British Museum, pp. 21, 22; © Sarah Gaunt/Champagne and Aishihik First Nations, p. 23; G. Fornaciari and L. Capasso, p. 25 (left); Dr. A. C. Aufderheide, University of Minnesota, Duluth, pp. 25 (right), 36 (left); Markus White/Historic St. Mary's City Commission, p. 26; © Paul Hanny/Liaison Agency, p. 27 (bottom); Dieter zur Nedden, p. 28 (top); © Maria Stenzel/National Geographic Image Collection, p. 35; Dr. Elliot Fishman, Johns Hopkins Hospital, p. 35 (inset); © Peter Menzel, p. 36 (right); Johan V. Hultin, pp. 37, 38 (both); © Enrico Ferorelli, pp. 39, 40, 41; Jeffery Newbury/©1994. Reprinted with permission of Discover Magazine, p. 44; © Reza Deghati/National Geographic Image Collection, p. 45 (both); Neg. no. 127468, photo by E. H. Morris, courtesy Department of Library Services, American Museum of Natural History, p. 46; Liaison Agency, p. 47; Sgt. Scott Seyer/Air Force News Agency/www.af.mil/news, p. 48; Kansas State Historical Society, p. 49 (bottom left); Scott Williams, The Salina Journal, p. 49 (top right); David R. Hunt, Anthropology, National Museum of Natural History, Smithsonian Institution, p. 50 (both); Ye Olde Curiosity Shop, p. 52; Western History Collections, University of Oklahoma Libraries, p. 53; Institut fur Plastination, Heidelberg, Germany, pp. 54, 55, 56.

Front cover: © Stephen Alvarez
Back cover: © Kenneth Garrett
Designed by Michael Tacheny

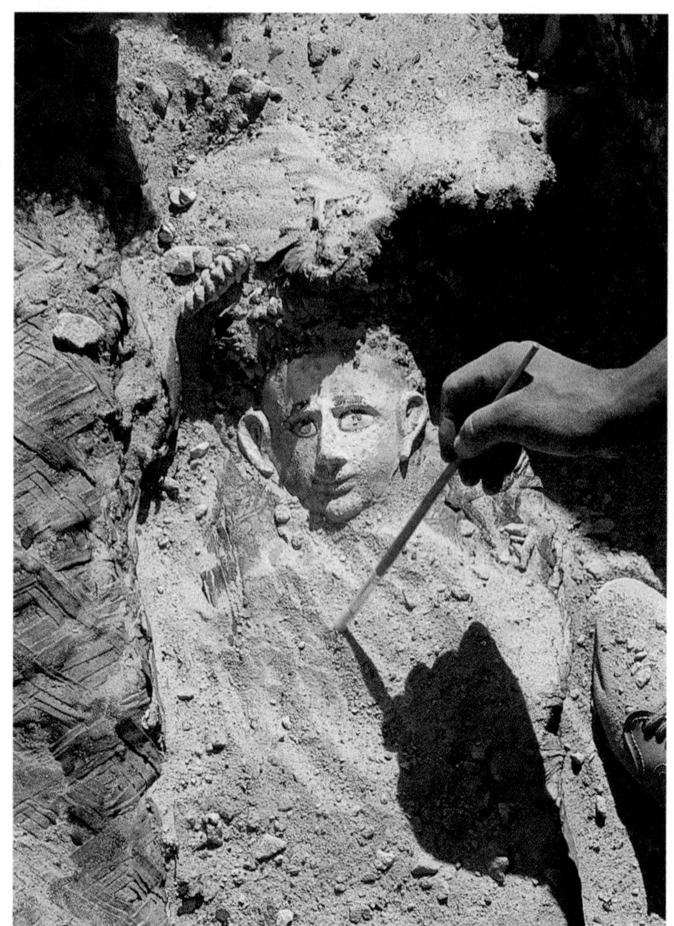

An archaeologist dusts off the face mask of the mummy of an Egyptian child buried at the Bahariya Oasis.

EDITOR: MARTIN WINDROW

OSPREY MILITARY
MEN-AT-ARMS SERIES 137

THE SCYTHIANS 700-300BC

Text by
Dr E V CERNENKO
Colour plates by
ANGUS McBRIDE
from reconstructions by
Dr M V GORELIK

First published in Great Britain in 1983 by
Osprey, an imprint of Reed Consumer Books Ltd.
Michelin House, 81 Fulham Road,
London SW3 6RB
and Auckland, Melbourne, Singapore and Toronto

Reprinted 1983, 1985, 1986, 1987, 1988, 1991, 1993, 1994,
1996

British Library Cataloguing in Publication Data

Cernenko, E. V.
The Scythians, 700–300 B.C.—(Men-at-Arms series; 137)
1. Scythians
I. Title II. Gorelik, M. V. III. Series
939·55 DK34.S4

ISBN 0–85045–478–6

Filmset in Great Britain
Printed through World Print Ltd, Hong Kong

Editor's note
Authors, illustrator and editor are pleased to record their gratitude to Dr. Heinrich Härke for his invaluable help, without which this book could not have been published, and to Dr. Michael Vickers for his prompt assistance.

Introduction

he text which follows is a translation from the Russian ·ginal commissioned by Osprey from the distinguished viet archaeologist Dr. E. V. Cernenko, of the Archae- ·gical Institute of the Academy of Sciences of the krainian SSR. The acting head of that institute's Scythian epartment, Dr. Cernenko has been active in the excavation Scythian tombs for many years. The colour plates by ıgus McBride are based upon reconstructions prepared for ·s book by Dr. M. V. Gorelik of the Oriental Institute of · Academy of Sciences of the SSSR, Moscow. Much of the ·itten and pictorial material in this book is published here · the first time in the West.

Although little known to non-specialists in this period d region, the Scythians were a dominant influence in uth-East Europe and the Middle East for more than three ıturies, being roughly contemporaneous with the Classical ·eek world. They were the first of the great armies of horse- chers out of the East which were to have such an impact on the consciousness of Europe at intervals over about ɔoo years. Yet they were not, like the Huns and Mongols, Turco-Mongoloid race, but straight-featured Indo- ıropeans: we know this from surviving pictorial metal- ɔrk, and from the few scraps of their language which come wn to us through the Greek historians.

Their mastery of the horse and the bow raised them from · obscurity of nomadic stock-raisers of the steppes to the ıtus of a major military power. At different periods they ushed—hard, and bruisingly—against the Assyrians, the ledes, the Persians, and the Macedonians. In the centuries their greatness they ruled a huge area of what is now the ·viet Union; interestingly, they seem to have retained their madic ways, while establishing an apparently stable lationship with the vassal communities of settled farmers ɔm whom they took tribute in a systematic way.

Although they left no written record, we know more of the ·bits and appearance of the Scythians than we do of many ɔre recent cultures. The southern part of their range met the rthern limits of the Greek world in the Greek trading cities ɔng the north shores of the Black Sea; and it was here that Herodotus, 'father of history', gathered the impressions of them which are still today our major written source. Here, also, they encountered skilled Greek metalsmiths. It is our good fortune that these violent, colourful, hard-drinking barbarians had a great love of decorative work in precious metals; a great wealth of such metals; the good taste to commission Greek master-craftsmen; and funerary customs which have preserved these precious relics for the study of the historian.

The Editor

The Scythians lived in the Early Iron Age, and inhabited the northern areas of the Black Sea (Pontic) steppes. Though the 'Scythian period' in the history of Eastern Europe lasted little more than 400 years, from the 7th to the 3rd centuries BC, the impression these horsemen made upon the history of their times was such that a thousand years after they had ceased to exist as a sovereign people, their

Sketch of the contents of a Scythian warrior's burial mound opened in the Nikolaev region. Dating from the 5th century BC, the tomb contains a complete suit of scale armour, including a helmet and leggings: cf. Plate D.

Comparative chronology of principal events in Scythian and Greek history

Scythians	*Greeks*
c.3200 BC Horse domesticated in southern Russia	
c.1500 BC Steppes inhabited by semi-nomadic horse-breeding tribes	
Early 7th C. BC Cimmerian and Scythian conquest of Urartu; Scythian activity in Middle East recorded in Assyrian texts	**7th C. BC** Poetry of Hesiod
670s BC Scythian king Partatua fights Assyria, marries daughter of Assyrian ruler Esarhaddon	**c.664 BC** First recorded naval engagement, between Corinth and Corcyra (Corfu)
Mid-7th C. BC King Madyes leads Scythian expedition to borders of Egypt	
c.652–626 BC Period of Scythian influence in Media	**640s BC** Poetry of Archilochus; first minting of coins in Asia Minor
	621 BC Draconian laws in Athens
612 BC Medes and Scythians capture Nineveh and destroy Assyrian Empire	
Late 7th C. BC Medes drive Scythians north of Caucasus into north Pontic area	
Early 6th C. BC Scythian philosopher Anacharsis travels in Greece	**594 BC** Solonian laws in Athens

Scythians	*Greeks*
	519 BC Athens and Plataea d feat Thebes
c.514–512 BC Scythians repel Persian invasion of south Russia under Darius the Great	**511 BC** Spartan campaig against Athens
c.496 BC Scythian expedition to Chersonesus in Thrace	**Early 5th C. BC** Writings of Aeschylus
Late 490s BC Scythians negotiate alliance against Persia with Spartan king Cleomenes I	**490 BC** Battle of Marathon
	480 BC Battles of Thermopyl and Salamis
Mid-5th C. BC Reign of King Scyles	**c.450 BC** Herodotus visits tradi colony at Olbia and r cords description Scythians
c.350 BC Beginning of Sarmatian expansion into Scythian territory	**c.437 BC** Pericles sends exp dition to Black Sea ar
339 BC Scytho-Macedonian war: King Atheas killed in battle with forces of Philip II in Rumania	**338 BC** Philip II defeats Athe and Thebes at Cha ronea
330 BC Alexander's general Zopyrion is routed by Scythians near Olbia	**323 BC** Death of Alexander tl Great
310–309 BC Scythians defeat Caucasians at Thatis River	
c.200 BC Scythians gradually withdraw into Crimea	
110–106 BC Scythians defeated in Crimea by King Mithridates Eupator of Pontus (Bosphoran kingdom)	

artland and the territories which they dominated
r beyond it continued to be known as 'greater
ythia'.

From the very beginnings of their emergence on
e world scene the Scythians took part in the
eatest campaigns of their times, defeating such
ighty contemporaries as Assyria, Urartu, Baby-
nia, Media and Persia.

The ancient Greek historian Herodotus recorded
at Cimmerian tribes had inhabited the Black Sea
eppes before the Scythians. Then came the
ythians, and conquered the Cimmerians. Pur-
ed by the Scythians, Cimmerian nomads crossed
e Caucasus and spread into the countries of
estern Asia; and the pursuing Scythians, led over
e mountains by their king Madyes, defeated the
edes they found in their path.

Early in the 7th century the Scythians moved
ainst Assyria. The official records of Assyria are
ghly selective, giving much space to Assyrian
ctories but remaining silent about Assyrian
efeats. Fortunately, a more balanced picture can
e built up by comparing various surviving
urces—not only the official record, but also the
ports of spies, and the questions put by Assyrian
ngs to oracles when seeking advice.

After a period of warfare between the Scythians
nd Assyrians the politically skilled Assyrian king
sarhaddon succeeded in winning peace with them,
r a time, by the presentation of rich gifts, and by
arrying off his daughter to the Scythian king
artatua. The Scythians' attentions were diverted
wards Palestine and Egypt. A Biblical prophet
ferred to the Scythians as 'the ancient, mighty
eople whose language is hard to understand. They
re always courageous, and their quivers are like an
pen grave. They will eat your harvest and bread,
ey will eat your sons and daughters, they will eat
our sheep and oxen, they will eat your grapes and
gs.' Only by paying heavy tribute did the Pharaoh
sammetichus I (reigned 663–609) save his country
om Scythian invasion.

From Egypt the Scythians returned to Assyria,
nd in the period *c.* 650–620 BC Media, one of the
chest states of the ancient East, fell steadily under
eir influence. In 612 BC a Scytho–Median army
nally captured Nineveh and overthrew the As-
rian Empire.

Herodotus says of the Scythian dominance of
Asia: 'The Scythians ravaged the whole of Asia. They not only took tribute from each people, but also made raids and pillaged everything these peoples had. Once Kiaksar and the Medians invited the Scythians to a feast, and killed them.' This suggests that the Scythian leadership were annihilated by treachery. At any event, the bulk of the nomad army drifted back north of the Caucasus at the end of the 7th century.

Much remains unclear, however, about the campaigns of the Scythians in the Middle East. It is not known whether they came south as disorganised nomad bands of plunderers, each following the tales of rich pickings which may have drifted back in the wake of the first bands to make the journey; or as a unified people with a disciplined 'state' army. We are also ignorant of the extent to which they returned to the Black Sea steppes, or remained in the Middle East.

Undoubtedly, they learned a lot from contact with the progressive civilisations of the Middle East. In the realm of warcraft, they learned how to fight effectively against cavalry and infantry alike, how to fight mounted and dismounted, and how to take well-fortified cities by storm. Bravery and a warlike nature alone would not have enabled them to defeat powerful and sophisticated ancient empires.

Of great importance, obviously, were the weapons and armour which enabled the warrior to strike down his enemy while protecting himself and his horse. The complex of Scythian war-gear was formed, by experience and by imitation, during their great campaigns in the Middle East; before this period the Scythians did not use defensive armour. Our knowledge of their weapons and armour comes from their funerary customs. Scythian dead were buried in barrow-mounds ('kurgans'), and the warrior was accompanied on his journey into eternity by the possessions which were most important to him in life. Rich finds of weapons and armour of many kinds have rewarded the excavation of Scythian barrows, including the tombs of many Scythian women. The grave of a common warrior usually contained a bow and several dozen arrows, and a pair of spears or a spear and a javelin. Royal tombs often yield whole arsenals of defensive armour, helmets, swords, quivers of arrows, dozens of spears, and—in the early period—large numbers of horse skeletons.

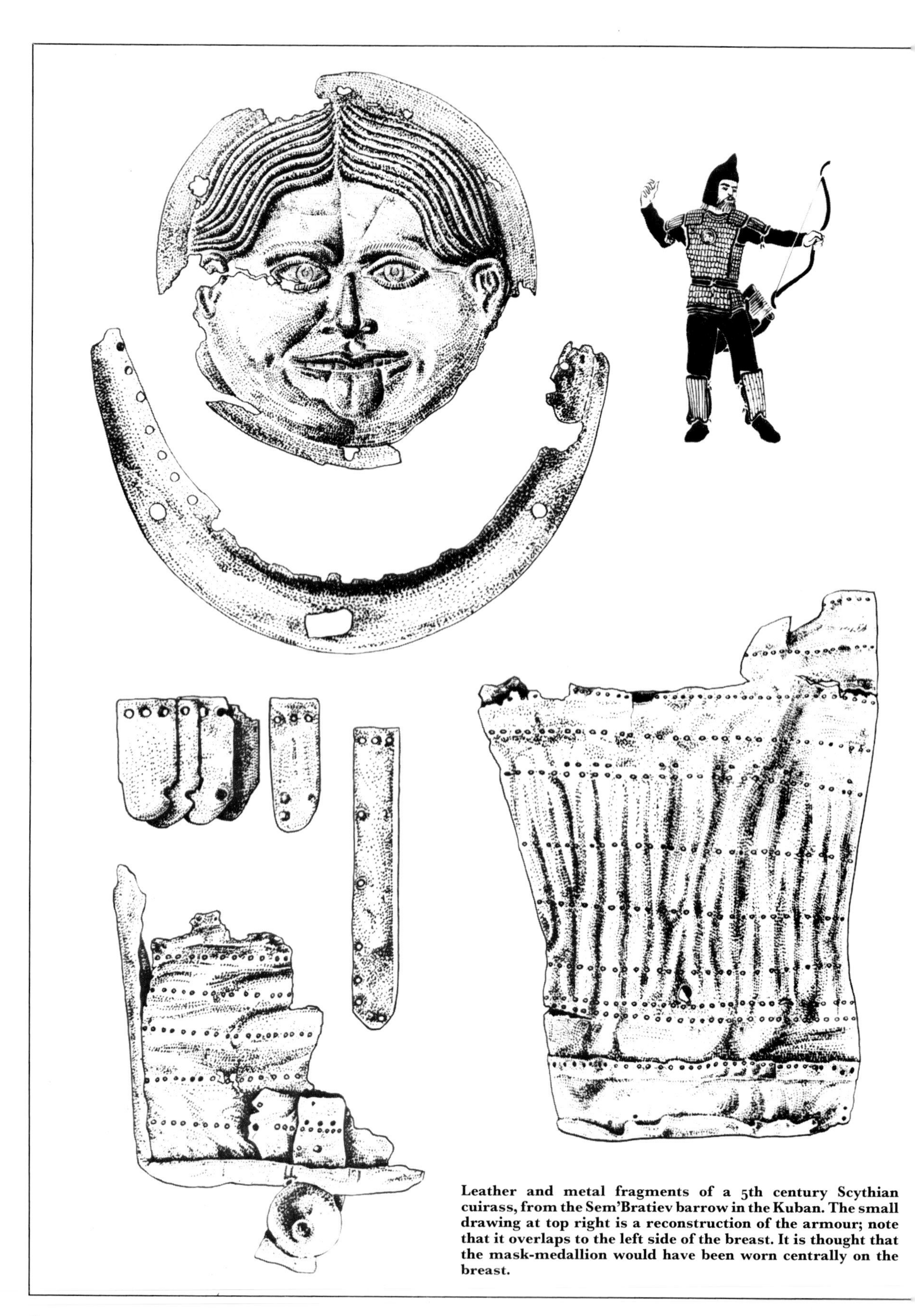

Leather and metal fragments of a 5th century Scythian cuirass, from the Sem'Bratiev barrow in the Kuban. The small drawing at top right is a reconstruction of the armour; note that it overlaps to the left side of the breast. It is thought that the mask-medallion would have been worn centrally on the breast.

Defensive Armour

exible leather corselets covered with small over-
pping scales of bronze or iron were worn in the
cient Middle East from about the middle of the
cond millenium before Christ. Quickly recognis-
g the advantage of a corselet proof against most
ord and spear-thrusts, the Scythians experimen-
d until they found the most efficient method of
ranging the overlapping 'fish-scales'. Remaining
use for thousands of years, the scale corselet ranks
a milestone in the development of the art of war
ongside the discovery and harnessing of bronze
d iron weapons, gunpowder and artillery.

The Scythians applied the same basic method to
her defensive armour. They covered helmets,
ields, girdles, and fabric clothing with small metal
ates, in contrast to the Middle Eastern smiths,
10 limited the use of scale to corselets. Scythian
mourers cut the scales from sheet metal with a
inted tool or shears; several dozen were needed to
shion a long-sleeved corselet. They were attached
a soft leather base by thin leather thongs or
imal tendons; each scale was set in such a way
at it covered one third or one half of the width of
e next scale sideways, and the row of plates
erlapped the one below it, protecting the stitch-
g where it was exposed in holes through the metal.
spear or arrow thus had to penetrate up to three
four basic scale thicknesses at most points on the
rface. Despite this excellent protection, the cor-
let did not greatly hinder the movements of the
ounted warrior; only ring-mail gave greater ease
manoeuvre.

These corselets, which gave the Scythian riders
otection from the earliest period of their military
eatness, varied in details of design. Some light-
ight types had metal scales only around the neck
d upper breast, or only on the front surface.
enerally the corselet resembled a short-sleeved
irt entirely covered with scales; we know of only a
w examples with long sleeves. The importance of
oulder protection in a mounted combat was
flected in many cases by the addition of a doubled
ke of scale-work across the upper back and
tending forward over the shoulders to the sides of
e breast. Ease of movement was preserved by
aking the corselet from different sizes of scales: small plates were used at elbow and shoulder, so as not to hinder arm movement, while the back and abdomen were covered with fewer, larger plates. As a rule the scales were of one metal only, usually iron; but we know of examples of corselets with different areas fashioned from iron and bronze: the spectacle must have been magnificent, as polished bronze glittered in the sun against the lustreless iron background. Finds from royal and noble tombs include corselets with each scale covered with fine gold leaf, and bronze scales decorated with figures of lions, deer, or elk heads.

The process of armour development was not entirely straightforward, however; and helmets provide us with an example of changing styles and materials. In the 6th century BC Scythian warriors wore heavy cast-bronze helmets, fitting tightly to the skull and protecting it part way down the face by means of cheek-pieces which left cut-outs for the eyes, and giving good protection to the back of the head. Many such helmets have been found in the Northern Caucasus, particularly in the Kuban area, where the most ancient graves have been discovered. (We may speculate that noblemen who took part in the Middle Eastern campaigns were buried here.) This style is popularly termed the 'Kuban helmet'.

From the 5th century onwards helmets of scale construction began to replace the 'Kuban' type. The pointed leather ('Phrygian') caps or hoods, commonplace among the Scythians, provided the model: they were covered with overlapping metal scales, and often had added cheek-pieces and neck-guards, a nasal being the only important element missing. Easy to make, they gave reliable protection against sword cuts. These helmets were in quite widespread use.

It was also in the 5th century that, among Scythian noblemen, the Greek helmet began to be worn; more than 60 bronze helmets made in Greece have been found in the richer Scythian barrows. These light, strong, beautiful pieces are generally of Corinthian, Chalcidian or Attic type.

The use of Scythian leg defences, of leather covered with metal plates, seems to have been at least partly replaced during the 5th century by Greek-style metal greaves. These may have been limited to heavy cavalry only. The armoured horseman of the 6th and early 5th centuries was

Part of an elaborately embossed Greek breastplate, from an armour discovered in a 4th century barrow in the Kuban. It is clear that there was much contact between the Scythians and the Greek communities on the northern Black Sea coast even before the rise of Macedon brought the two powers into confrontation.

characterised by iron-faced leggings; his successor of the late 5th and 4th century, by greaves worn over fabric trousers. Prosperous leaders sometimes had gilded greaves; and a superb pair found about 150 years ago and now in the Hermitage, Leningrad have Gorgon heads on the knee-pieces and pairs of snakes, tail down, worked down the sides. Our colour plates show some examples of Greek helmets and greaves, originally heavy infantry items, modified for use by Scythian heavy cavalry.

The Scythians placed importance on the shield and its decoration. While ordinary warriors seem to have used light shields of woven osiers—e.g. the example on the famous Solokha comb—the heavy cavalry carried more massive shields faced wi
iron. The classic construction was a wooden ba
faced with scales of iron, sewn to each other and
the backing with wire. There is evidence of son
use, presumably by the richer nobles, of shiel
completely faced with single, round iron plate
with applied decorative motifs of other metals. (It
thought that the scale-faced shields may also ha
borne such decorations on occasion.) Two go
decorative plates, more than 30cm long, were four
in the graves of early Scythian noblemen
Kostromskaya Stanistsa and Kelermes in th
Kuban; the former is in the shape of a deer, and th
latter, a panther, in the 'animal style' so typical
the Scythians. A bronze fish motif has also bee
found in a grave not far from the famous Tolstay
Mogila site, and a gold deer—showing strong Gree
influence—in the royal tomb at Kul Oba.

Another major category of Scythian defensi

Moscow
Volga River
Ural River
Dniepr River
Don River
SCYTHIANS
SARMATIANS
Kiev
Donets River
Dniestr River
Gaimonov
Melgunov
Chertomlyk
Solokha
SEA OF AZOV
Olbia
CASPIAN SEA
Prut River
Kul Oba
Kostromskaya
CARPATHIANS
Tyras
Kelermes
Kerch
CAUCASUS
Seven Brothers
BLACK SEA
Danube River
URARTU
THRACE
ASSYRIA
Nineveh
Athens
Tigris River
Euphrates River
Babylon
MEDITERRANEAN
SYRIA
EGYPT
Grave Finds
Modern Towns
Ancient Towns

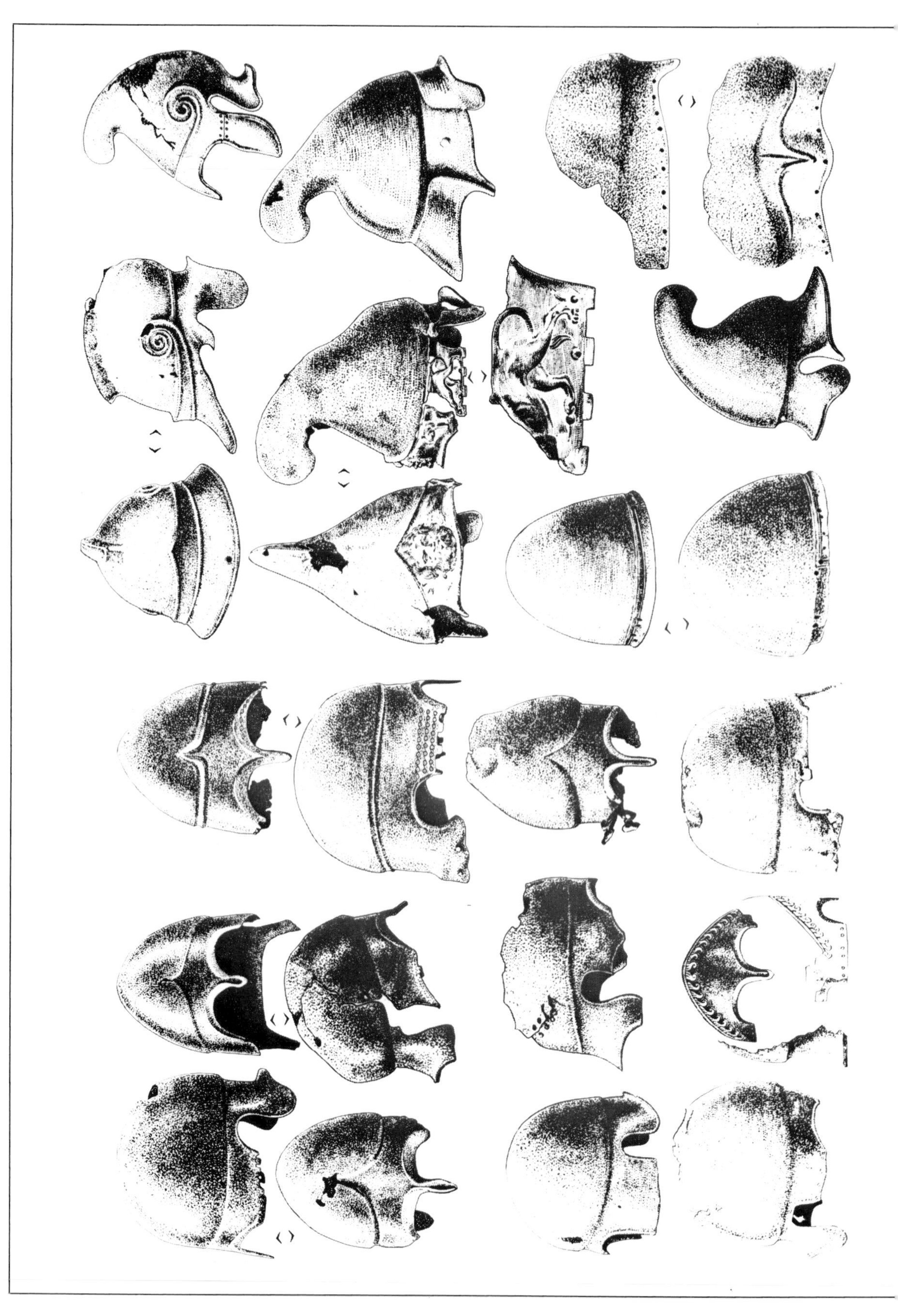

nour is the girdle, of leather faced with strips of 1, bronze, or even silver or gold. Typical of the ly period, and of dismounted warriors whose lomens were not protected by the neck of the se, these broad girdles often had several rows of les or strips. Narrow belts for the slinging of rds, daggers, battleaxes, bows and quivers, etstones and whips were also worn by the thians. The defensive girdle declined in size with passage of time, and was eventually 'absorbed' the increasingly common corselet.

Protection for the horse took several forms. Since 6th century BC metal plates and pendant orations on the bridle helped to protect the se's head and cheeks. There is evidence to port the use in some cases of a leather horse-cloth h attached metal scales, and a thick felt 'apron' the breast, in which the enemy's arrows became ck without penetrating.

'Kuban'-type Scythian bronze helmet found in the 6th century barrow at Kelermes (Stanitsa Kelermesskaya). See Plate A for reconstruction. Note the holes for attachment of an aventail; the raised ribs all round the lower edge and part way round the back of the skull; the raised flange at the brow, and the reinforcement running centrally over the skull to the point between the eyes.

Offensive Weapons

long-range fighting the Scythians used bows l slings; at intermediate range they employed ars and javelins; and for hand-to-hand combat, rds, axes, maces, and daggers.

ws and Arrows

ery Scythian had a bow and arrows; all male ves contain great numbers of arrowheads, and so about one in three of all female graves, and many ldren's graves. Arrowheads are found in the nbs of king and humble rider alike. The bow and ows accompanied the Scythian from cradle to ve, and beyond; it is clear that the Scythians ieved that the dead would need them to hunt l fight in the world beyond. Scythian ar-vheads can be found all over the Eurasian ppes, and the Scythian style of bow was in widespread use throughout Eastern Europe and Western and Central Asia.

Sadly, the materials used to make bows—wood, bone and animal tendons—perish easily, and only a few out of the 5,000 or so known Scythian graves contain identifiable remains of bows, and those so poorly preserved that it is almost impossible to reconstruct their original appearance with confidence. Luckily we can also study sculptural evidence, pictorial metalwork from grave finds, and the descriptions of ancient authors.

Surviving written descriptions compare the unstrung, recurved Scythian bow with the Greek letter *sigma* (Σ), or the Black Sea coastline. Ammianus Marcellinus wrote: 'While the bows of all peoples are made of flexible branches, Scythian bows . . . resemble the crescent moon, with both ends curved inwards'. The middle of the bow is described as a regular curve. This description corresponds well with the bows depicted on gold and silver bowls found in the graves of Scythian kings at Kul Oba and Voronezh. Only the grips and ends of bows have been preserved, the latter having decorative bone tips in the graves of some noblemen. Judging by pictures and the length of the arrows, the bow was quite short—up to 80cm; but as with all examples of the classic Eastern 'composite' bow, the

ek, Thracian and Macedonian helmets, and fragments of nets, all recovered from Scythian burial mounds. More n 60 have been found in Scythian burials, some in original dition and some apparently modified by local smiths: see te E. The three columns on the left are Attic, Chalcidian, perhaps remains of Corinthian types; those on the right Thracian, as favoured by the Macedonians—though note resting Thracian/Boeotian composite.

This helmet from the famous 4th century Solokha burial hoard seems to be of Greek manufacture—'Attic'-type?—with later modifications by Scythian armourers. Extra neck and cheek defences were sometimes added.

length of its cast was determined by its very taut compression rather than by its length of stave. Ancient authors write that the string was of horsehair or animal tendon.

The arrow shaft itself was of reed or a thin birch branch. The fletching was made conventionally from birds' feathers. The heads were of iron, bronze, or sometimes of bone. There were different types, apparently designed specifically for the hunt, or to pierce corselets, shields and helmets. The 'trilobate' arrowheads found in such numbers in the excavated tombs are of strict aerodynamic forms and superbly exact workmanship; the simplicity and perfection of their lines stands comparison with modern rockets.

The Scythian bow was capable of accuracy at considerable range. An old Greek grave found at Olbia, the ancient trading city on the Dniepr–Bug estuary, bears an inscription to the effect that Anaxagoras son of Dimagoras shot an arrow from his bow to a range of 282 *orgyiai* (521.6 metres). Since Olbians, like the inhabitants of other ancient cities on the Black Sea coast, favoured the Scythian bow, it is fair to assume that the archer achieved his feat with a weapon obtained from the steppe horsemen: a feat which is breathtaking even today.

Apparently, Scythians could match the rate of shooting recorded for skilled archers of the Middle Ages—between ten and 12 arrows a minute. The Scythian carried anything between 30 and 150 arrows into battle, and could expend them in three to 15 minutes' shooting. Given the hundreds of mounted archers who took part in most enga ments, one can only imagine the hail of dea arrows which fell among their enemies. T penetrative force of the arrows was also consid able. Some graves yield human skeletons w arrowheads embedded in the skull or spine to depth of two to three centimetres. Many pictures ancient cups and vessels show warriors in corsel pierced by arrows, or hoplite shields simila penetrated. Many authors of antiquity wrote t Scythian arrowheads were poisoned.

The Scythian bow was extremely stiff a powerful, and great strength and skill were need to string it. According to Herodotus, Heracles his bow to his sons when he set out from Scyth saying that only the son who could string it as he would rule the Black Sea steppes. The youngest s Scythes, succeeded, and Herodotus wrote that race of Scythians was descended from him. T legend may explain why scenes showing shooting of the bow, or the passing of a bow fr one warrior to another, or the stringing of the b occupy a prominent place in Scythian art.

The bow was carried in a special case slung fr the belt on campaign, and was only removed battle or the chase. In the pre-Scythian peri when the northern Black Sea steppes were habited by the Cimmerians, a case of simple fo was used. The Scythian case, called by the Gre a *gorytos*, held both the bow and up to 75 arro sadly, no complete example is known to survive, only rotten fragments of leather have been found graves. We know, however, that its length was t thirds that of the bow, and that the quiver sect had a metal-clasped cover. Early Scythian ton yield many bronze, bone, and even gold buckl

The quiver section was often covered with ornate gold facing plate decorated with figures deer; but since the plate covered only a part of gorytos, finds in early graves do not show us complete form of the case in this period. Only in 4th century BC did it become the fashion to face whole gorytos with metal plates. The first find this type was unearthed from the Chertomlyk ro tomb site. This large gold plate is covered with pl motifs, animals, figures of men, women and chi ren in Greek clothing, items of furniture, weapo and even architectural structures. For deca opinions differed about the significance of th strations; but it has now been established that y represent scenes from the *Iliad* of Homer, in rticular the visit of Achilles to the island of Skiros, d the story of how this was discovered by lysseus.

For nearly 50 years the Chertomlyk gorytos nained unique; then, three more gold facings re discovered, identical to the Chertomlyk ample. It is apparent that a master metalsmith, ssibly Greek, set up a workshop in one of the ythian centres, making a series of gold plates for vering the gorytos to the order of Scythian kings d nobles. Many must have been stolen from ves and melted down; doubtless many more nain in the ground, awaiting discovery.

Quite recently an interesting find was made ich proves the existence of another series of gold rytos used by prosperous leaders. A very rich acedonian royal grave, which had somehow aped plundering, was found at the site of a small eek settlement called Vergina. Amongst other items the archaeologists unearthed the remains of a gorytos which was identical to one found in a Scythian mound in the Northern Caucasus nearly 100 years ago. The Scythians combined bowcase and quiver was not used in Greece and Macedonia; how could this undoubtedly Scythian gorytos have found its way into the grave of a Macedonian nobleman—perhaps even Philip II himself?

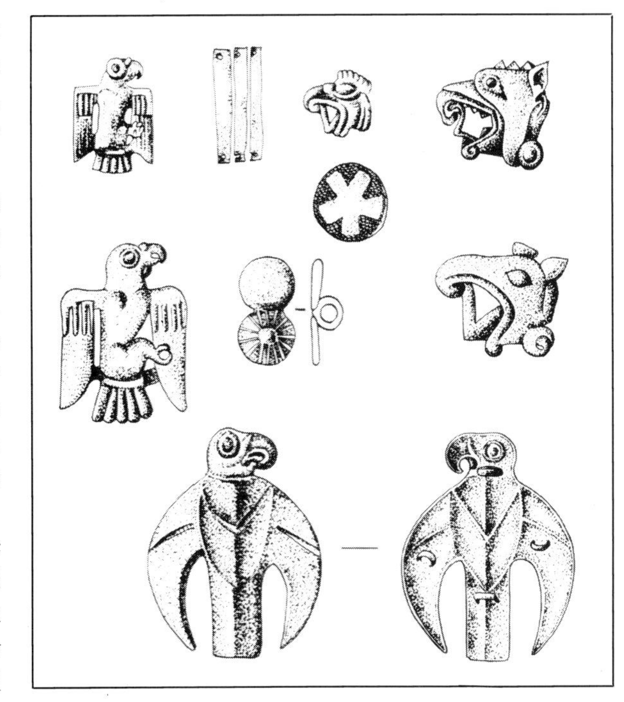

Various decorative plates and studs from Scythian belts, both everyday and ceremonial, recovered from burial sites of the 6th to 4th centuries. The Scythian love of animal motifs, the so-called 'feral' style of ornamentation, produced wonderfully vigorous images which remind us of the similar but distinct Scandinavian and Germanic styles of a thousand years later.

o different Greek greaves recovered from barrows on the rch peninsula. The beautiful workmanship of these exactly portioned defences is obvious even from these simple tches. The greaves split down the back centrally, and were d to the calf purely by the spring of the thinly-beaten metal. s not hard to see why the work of Greek armourers ealed to the Scythian nobility.

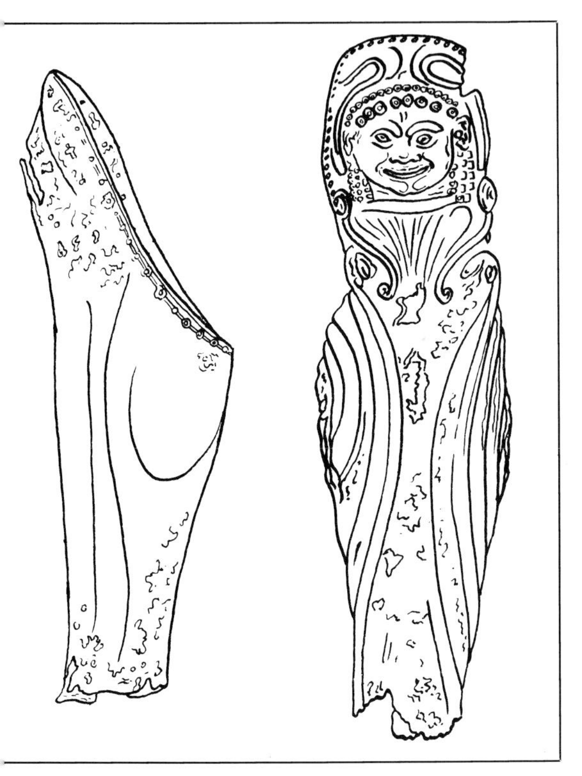

Shortly before this interment, negotiations took place between Philip of Macedon and the king of Scythia; they broke down without agreement being reached, and war broke out between the Scythians and Macedonians. In 339 BC the 90-year-old Scythian king Atheas was killed in battle with the Macedonians, who captured rich trophies. Apparently the gorytos found in the Macedonian grave was either part of the ritual exchange of gifts at the time of negotiation, or war booty. This example, and that from Karagodeuashkh in the Northern Caucasus, have similar forms to the Chertomlyk gorytos and to other finds from Scythian barrows; both show the assault and looting of a city, believed by scholars to be a representation of the fall of Troy.

One of the most famous of all Scythian finds: the golden comb, featuring a battle scene, from the 4th century Solokha royal burial mound.

A very interesting gorytos was found shortly before the First World War in the Scythian royal burial of Solokha. Generally similar to those described above, it bears a scene of special interest. Unlike other examples decorated with traditional animal motifs, ornamented gold or silver plates, or scenes of Classical warfare, the Solokha find shows episodes from the life of the Scythians. The central part is filled with a scene of three young Scythians on foot fighting two elderly Scythians on horseback. On the left is a young warrior armed with a battleaxe, carrying a shield and with a gorytos on his belt, who attacks a mounted Scythian armed with a spear. This rider is hurrying to the aid of a comrade-in-arms who has been attacked, dragged from his horse, and killed by two young men before having a chance to draw his sword. The elderly horseman seems certain to suffer defeat. This scene calls to mind a story told by Herodotus.

He writes that Scythian warriors setting off on campaign to western Asia left their wives in Scythia, together with many slaves. 'These slaves and the Scythian women gave birth to a younger generati of men, who determined to rise against the warri upon their return from Media. They dug a de moat from the Taurus Mountains [the Crime Mountains] to the Maeotic Lake [the Sea of Azo and when the returning warriors attempted to cr the moat the young men attacked them. The elc Scythians were at first unable to defeat them. Th one warrior exclaimed: "What are we doing? fighting against them we deplete both our o forces and the number of our slaves. Let us drop c spears and bows and take up whips. Seeing weapon in hand, they imagined that they were c equals, and of the same noble origins. But wh they see us with whips instead of weapons they w understand that they are only our slaves, and w not be able to resist us". The Scythians followed t advice, and the slaves, astonished, forgot abc fighting and took flight. Thus the Scythia returned to their homes.'

Apparently, the Solokha gorytos shows an e sode from the early stages of the battle between t veterans and the young men.

It is notable that although the use of the quiv for arrows alone, was very widespread in t ancient Middle East, no single example among t dozens of surviving sculptures and pictorial me objects showing Scythians includes a quiver; t combined bow and arrow case is universal.

The sling seems also to have been a popu weapon among the Scythians, and many gra contain several dozen sling-stones—in one case, many as 75.

Swords and Daggers

The sword and dagger also play an important pa in the culture of the Scythians. The ancient Gre traveller, historian and geographer Herodot whose notes taken during a visit to the Black S region in the 5th century remain our major writt source, wrote that 'Ares, the God of War, was t only deity whom the Scythians worshipped and whom they built altars'. The war-god embodied t fortune of war. Every region of Scythia had a lar mound made of brushwood. 'An old iron sword w placed on top of each mound. That was an altar the God of War, to whom more sacrifices we offered than to any other god. Every year th brought cattle and horses to these swords. Fr ong captured enemies they sacrificed every ndredth man. First a libation of wine was poured er their heads. Then they cut their victims' throats d collected the blood, and carried it to the top of mound and poured it over the sword. At the foot he altar they cut the right arm and shoulder from body, and tossed them in the air, each arm being to lie where it fell. The trunks lay separately.'

Herodotus's story was confirmed by the archae-gical excavations near Zaporozhye. It was hard the Scythians to make the mounds of brushwood nanded by tradition, living as they did on the nost treeless steppes. Mounds of sand were raised tead; and it was one of these which was covered near Zaporozhye, surrounded by grave-unds dating back to the 4th century. The altar elf was at least a hundred years older, since the ord found at its top dates from the 5th century.

The origins of the Scythian sword are still not irely clear, but mounting material evidence nts towards the weapons carried by their decessors on the steppes, the Cimmerians. By late in the 7th century the form of the Scythian sword was established. In its earliest examples it has a two-edged, almost parallel-sided blade tapering at the point, about 60–70cm long—though a single example of a huge sword with a blade one metre long, dated to the 6th century, has been found in the Crimea. Daggers, of similar shape, were generally 35–40cm long.

The most ancient finds come from the late 7th/early 6th century mounds at Melgunov and Kelermes. The two swords are very alike, differing only in secondary details: so much alike, indeed, that they may have been modelled on the same standard pattern, perhaps even in the same smithy. Each is decorated with thin gold plates fixed round

Detail from the Solokha comb: note the evident mixture of Greek and Scythian war-gear worn by the mounted warrior, who has a Corinthian helmet, and muscled greaves sprung over his Scythian trousers. The cuirass and girdle are Scythian. The crescent-shaped shield is a common image in Pontic art; the footsoldier who bears it wears highly decorated clothing, a sword interestingly and untypically slung on the left hip in the position normally occupied by the gorytos, and what seems to be the typical Scythian cap.

Detail from the Solokha comb: the shield is reconstructe Plate F.

Detail from the Solokha comb: the Greek linen cuirass, added scale protection on the breast, tied-down shoulder y and 'feathered' skirt, could hardly be clearer.

the hilt and scabbard, on which fine geometr patterns and animal forms are stamped. animals are both real—deer, goats, lions— mythical—various combinations of the goat, l bull, fish, and human archer. Both swords featu scene of winged gods standing around a sacred t It is quite obvious that the ornamentation has uniformity of style. The craftsman's manner quaint mixture of different styles from Urartu present-day Armenia), Assyria and Media. Som the animal forms decorating the scabbards, e.g. deer and mountain goat, were later to bec typical of Scythian art, however.

These swords were brought back by Scythians from their conquests in the Middle and Asia Minor. It is natural that local smi producing goods to the order of their Scyth upiers, should blend the artistic styles of different tures into a curious whole.

Vith the passage of time, the Scythian sword nged shape. The 5th century saw the parallel-d blade replaced by an elongated isosceles ngle with a continuous taper down its whole gth; and in the 4th century single-edged blades peared beside the double-edged. During the century the pommel changed from a simple ssbar shape to a more complex fashion, with two ons' of iron rising and curling inwards. In the rse of the 4th century the pommel tended to ert to a simpler oval shape; the grip, too, nged, from a cylindrical to a double-tapered or l shape much more convenient to the hand. The rd took on a triangular shape, with a sharp, ved indent in the centre of the bottom edge. The ompanying photographs illustrate these points re clearly than words.

The scabbard was made of wood covered with ther, throughout Scythian history. It hung from belt by a thong passing through its projecting r', and various sculptural finds indicate that it s worn well forward on the right side of the lomen. Some of our colour plates show how this ght have worked in practice for a horseman.

A curious find was recently made in a grave-und at Belozerka near Zaporozhye, unlike thing previously recorded by archaeologists. e tribesmen who were burying their comrade 23 turies ago had made a deep, narrow hole in the or of the barrow, and had inserted a sword into it nt downwards, the pommel being barely visible ove the floor-level. The sword was a 'dress' or emonial one, its hilt and scabbard sheathed in n gold plate. On the scabbard were illustrations oredatory animals clawing their prey—a popular thian motif. A lion and a griffon pounce on a r; two panthers race alone, wiry and menacing. the protruding 'ear' of the scabbard is a superb d of a wild boar, the Greek letters 'πOP' cut in forehead.

The interest lies not only in the curious method of rial, but also in the fact that similar scenes are nd on the sword from the famous barrow of l Oba, excavated nearly 150 years ago on the tskirts of Kerch. The ornamentation of the l Oba scabbard has much in common with the ozerka find; while the 'ears' have different motifs, the main five-figured scenes are literally identical, having been embossed into the plate with the same stamp. (The Belozerka sword is shorter than that from Kul Oba, which explains why some scenes from the latter are missing from the former.) This appears to be convincing proof of the existence of armourers' shops on the north coast of the Black Sea, probably in Panticapaeum or some other city of the kingdom of Bosphorus, which then ran along the coast of the strait and peninsula of Kerch.

Until recently it was thought that the great majority of Scythian swords were short; but increasing numbers of finds of longer blades have changed our view of Scythian tactics, since long swords would naturally allow a greater tactical flexibility in the use of mounted men against both infantry and cavalry.

Spears, Javelins and Axes

Many spears and javelins were used by the Scythians, and one or two are found beside almost every buried warrior. Some barrows contain much greater numbers: more than ten were found in the Scythian royal barrow near Berdyansk on the Sea of Azov.

Until recently historians believed that the Scythians used only short spears or javelins, which could be either thrown or wielded in close combat; this stemmed from the simple fact that Scythian burial chambers are too short for a longer weapon. That a spear might be broken before being laid in the grave did not occur to anyone until attention was drawn to the relationship of points and shafts as they were found lying in a number of tombs. It has now become clear that some of the Scythian spears are more properly termed lances, since they were more than three metres long and obviously intended for mounted combat.

Shorter spears, about 1.7–1.8 metres long, were used both for throwing and for thrusting, and from pictorial evidence on funerary finds in rich Scythian burial mounds it is clear that they were used equally for war and for the chase. Thrown by a trained hand, such spears could kill or wound at ranges up to 30 metres. Spearheads of both long and short types come in various forms, usually leaf-shaped, with a central spine for added strength and a socket for the shaft. Length varies greatly, from 30 to 72cm, and the longer heads were presumably for

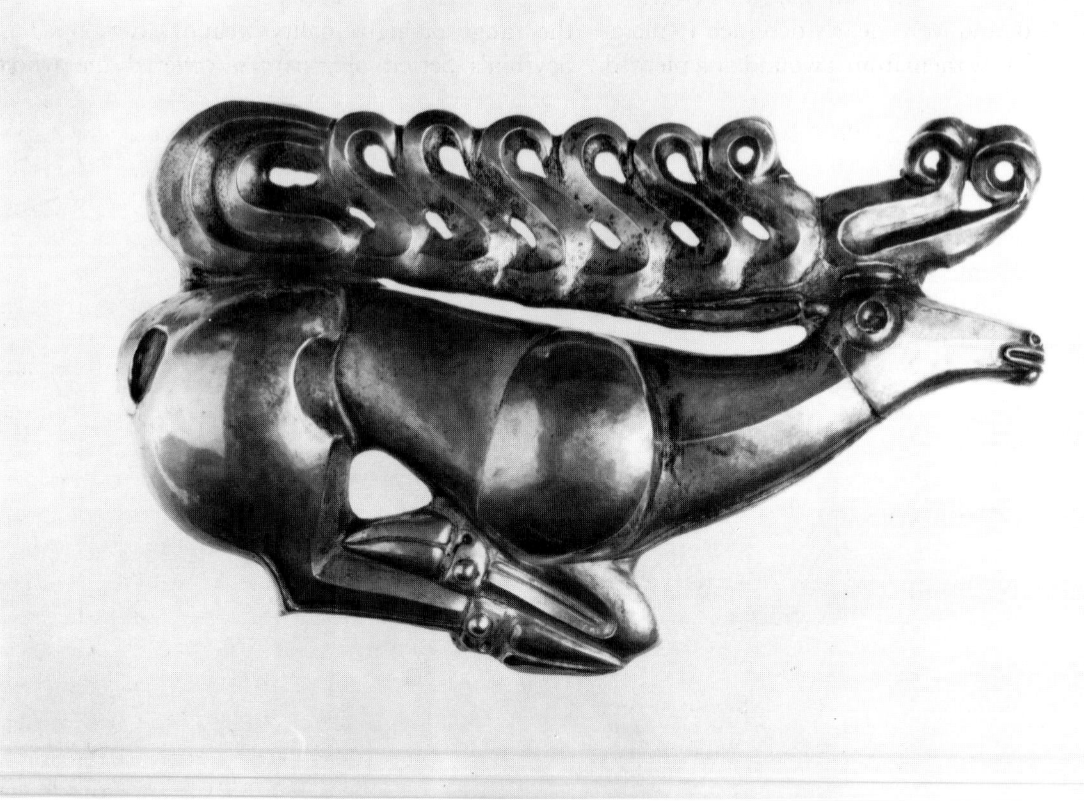

sier penetration of armour. Ferrules from the butt
ds of shafts have also been found.

Javelins intended solely for missile use, or 'darts',
d heads of an entirely different form. They had a
ng iron shank with a small pyramidal head,
arply barbed, and were clearly designed to make
hard to withdraw them from a wound or a pierced
eld.

Nearly a hundred iron battleaxes of various types
ve been found in the burial mounds excavated in
mer Scythian territories. One magnificent speci-
en was recovered from the famous Kelermes
rrow, covered entirely with gold plate except for
narrow 'tomahawk' blade. The ornamentation
mbines a number of styles. The blade has
graved forms of mountain goats and deer; more
ats adorn the head, and the gold-covered shaft
esents a stunning pattern of mingled figures of
l and mythical beasts, birds and insects.

Elegant maces with lobed heads served not only
weapons but also as symbols of authority. A fine
ecimen was found in the Solokha barrow. The
companying photographs illustrate this and the

T:
**e 6th century Kelermes mound yielded this shield dec-
tion in the shape of a lioness or panther; and the deer came
m the Kostromskaya burial. Of solid gold and more than
m long, these pieces are superb examples of the Scythian
imal style.**

Decorative and defensive bridle fittings recovered from Scythian barrows of the 5th to 4th centuries BC.

other types of weapons described above.

To summarise, one can state with confidence that the range of high-quality weapons developed in Scythia's period of greatness covered the whole spectrum of pre-gunpowder armament, and equipped her warriors for every type of mounted and dismounted combat against every kind of enemy. Throughout the subsequent history of arms, only the sabre and the ring-mail body-armour represent types not already introduced and mastered by the Scythians—and there is even some evidence that they made use of ring-mail.

Most Scythian weapons and armour were made by native smiths, using great quantities of local or imported iron and bronze, and working them to a high standard of craftsmanship. For the richest members of Scythian society, magnificent ceremonial weapons were made by Greek armourers in the trading cities along the north Pontic coast, combining Scythian styles of decoration with Greek craftsmanship in silver and gold to produce genuine masterpieces of the metalsmith's art. Safe within the burial mounds of their owners, these richly decorated weapons, cuirasses and shields have survived the ravages of the centuries to adorn the world's finest museum collections. Scythian achievements in weaponry are thought to have had a considerable influence on the development of arms in neighbouring lands. The Greeks of the Pontic colonies adopted the full range of Scythian weapons in preference to their own, and Scythian-made weaponry has been found thousands of kilometres to the north, west and east of Scythia, as far as the Arctic Circle, Germany and Mongolia.

The Scythian Army

It is difficult to reconstruct the organisation of the Scythian army. Written sources confirm its division into cavalry and infantry, and this is not contradicted by archaeological data. Cavalry was the principle arm of the Scythians, as was typically the case among nomadic societies. Herodotus and Thucydides put it in a clear-cut way, stating that each Scythian warrior was a mounted archer. On the other hand, Diodorus Siculus wrote that in one particular battle the Scythians fielded twice as many foot as horse. This is not surprising, in fact; for Diodorus was dealing with events of the late 4th century, when the gradual transition from nomadic to sedentary life among the Scythians was becoming marked; and it should also be noted that the majority of the combatants in the battle he describes were drawn from areas where this process was especially advanced.

Throughout early Scythian history the overwhelming majority of the men were mounted; infantry consisted of the poorer Scythians, and levies from those settled tribes whose territory was now dominated by the Scythians. Commoners from these vassal tribes, which were obliged to provide military service, served on foot, and their more well-to-do leaders in the cavalry.

The bulk of the cavalry was probably made up of lightly-armed warriors, protected by no more than fur or hide jackets and headgear. The shock force of the Scythian host was the professional, heavily-armed cavalry commanded by local princes. Both horses and riders were well protected. They fought in formation, under discipline, and brought to the battlefield considerable experience of warfare. The engagement opened with a shower of arrows a sling-stones, followed at closer range by darts a javelins. The heavy cavalry then charged in cl formation, delivering the main blow on the centre the enemy's array. They were certainly capable manoeuvre in battle, breaking through the ene ranks, regrouping in the thick of the action, a changing direction to strike at the right place at t right time. When the enemy had been broken t lightly-armed mass of the Scythian horse closed to finish them off.

Almost the whole of the adult population Scythia, including a large number of the wom folk, fought on campaign. It is impossible estimate the numbers of soldiers Scythia could p into the field simultaneously; Scythian kings the selves wished that they knew. Herodotus tells us King Ariantes, who attempted to establish t numbers of his subjects by ordering every Scythia on pain of death, to bring one arrowhead to t muster. So many arrowheads were brought that decided to have a monument made of them. bronze vessel cast from the melted-down metal w reputed to contain 600 *amphorae*, with walls fingers thick; at the standard Attic measure, t represents 23,400 litres (5,200 gallons).

Thucydides wrote that the Scythian army w larger than a 150,000-strong Thracian tribal ho

A gold decorative plaque showing Scythian archers, from 4th century Kul Oba burial. Note fur-trimmed jackets, corated trousers, and short boots. The top-knot hairstyle Plate B) is unusual in Scythian pictorial work. The sho sharply recurved bows are accentuated here.

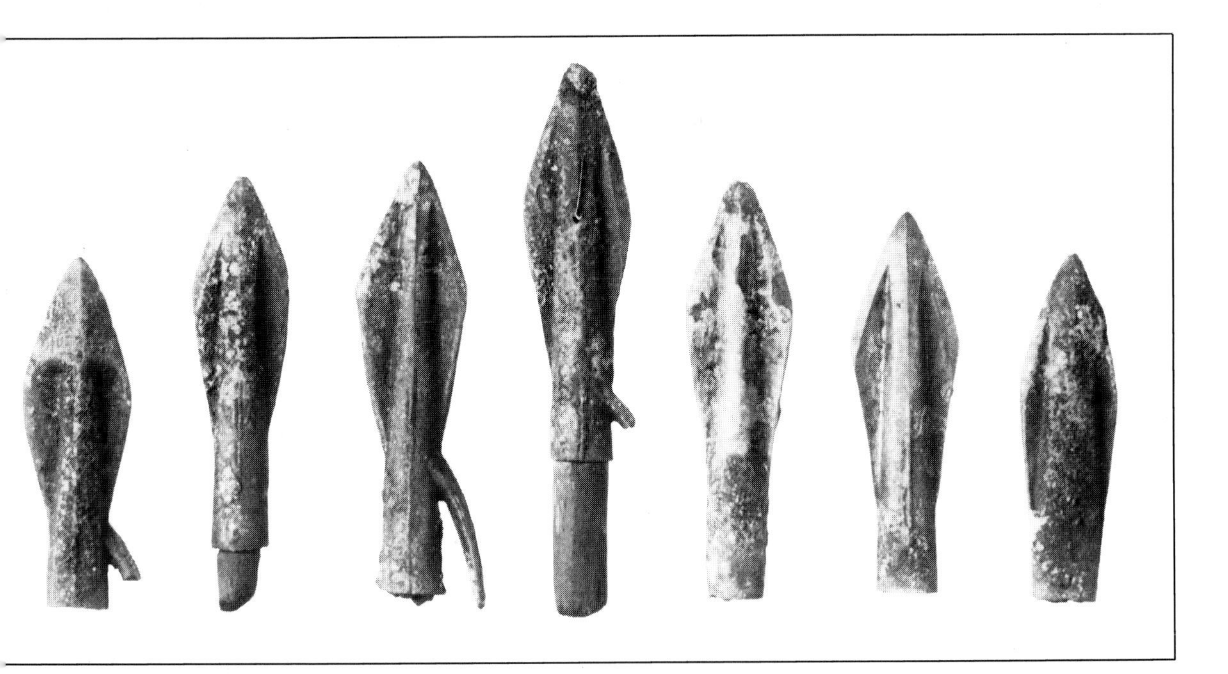

Bronze Scythian arrowheads from a 4th century burial near Kiev. Note the long single barb on three of these pieces.

.d that not one people in Europe or Asia could sist the Scythians unaided, if the Scythians were .l of one will'. This comment draws attention to e traditional nature of nomadic tribal societies, iose strength is normally fairly widely dispersed in ore or less independent groups, and which can .dom if ever bring their whole strength into the ld together. Against this, one must remember at Scythia was a military state, whose entire social ucture was geared to the needs of war; one might rrow the words of the mighty Persian king arius the Great about the Persian nation, d term the Scythians 'a people at arms'.

The Persian Invasion

ore than a hundred years had passed since the ythians returned to the steppes north of the Black a and the Caucasus from their conquests in the iddle East. All veterans of those campaigns were ng dead of their wounds or old age, and laid to rest der their grassy barrows; but in the fortresses and wns of Armenia, Syria, Palestine, and even ıbylon, the terrible memories of their war-cries d their whistling arrows were still green. In ythia, old warriors recounted their grandfathers' orious feats of arms in faraway lands to the young bloods gathered round them. In an oral society the names of kings and the exact order of events would fade gently into legend; but the legend would live on.

But now the half-forgotten past threatened to strike back, and dark clouds gathered over the broad plains of Scythia. In more than one hundred years of her vigour she had invaded many neighbouring lands; now, it seemed, Scythia would pay in her turn. A formidable enemy was preparing to invade the Pontic steppes, claiming justification in the wars of long ago. The enemy was none other than the Great King of Persia, Darius I Hystaspes of the Achaemenid dynasty.

Towards the end of the 6th century BC Darius I had managed to create a mighty state, the most powerful nation on earth at that time. His empire stretched from Egypt to India. Preparing for future conquests, he increased his power by introducing a number of reforms, and created a strong army. Since the Greek city-states stood in his path westwards, they would be conquered. But before he could move against them the empire's northern marches must be made safe from possible new inroads by the nomads of the steppes—the Scythians, and their neighbours the Sauromatae. We owe most of what we know of the events which

This magnificent gold vessel from the Kul Oba royal tomb shows many details of Scythian costume. This warrior is stringing his bow, bracing it behind his knee; note the typical pointed cap or hood, long jacket with fur or fleece trimming at the edges, decorated trousers, and short boots tied at t ankle. The hair seems normally to have been worn long a loose, and beards were apparently worn by all adult men.

lowed to Herodotus and to other ancient Greek d Roman authors.

Before invading Scythia the Persians carried out reconnaissance in force. Ariaramnes, the ruler of e of the satrapies, led northwards a fleet of 100 ips; he landed on the Scythian coast and probed land, taking many prisoners—among them, ood-brothers of the Scythian king. This evidence Darius's warlike intentions was soon confirmed. erodotus tells us that he sent messengers to his ssal states, with orders to contribute levies to the my and the fleet, and to build a bridge across the ellespont, which was known as the Thracian sphorus at this period. Within a relatively short ne he mustered forces estimated by Herodotus at 0,000 men, and by other authors at the even more ntastic figure of 800,000. The real number was rtainly much smaller, as was the number of ips—600, if one is to believe Herodotus. Neverеless, though we cannot venture an estimate of r own, this was certainly one of the greatest mies of antiquity.

Crossing the bridge of boats over the Hellespont, this enormous force broke through the resistance of the Thracian tribes without difficulty. By the spring or summer of 512 BC Darius had reached the Danube, which was also bridged by anchoring ships across its span. The mighty army of invasion began to roll across to the left bank of the river onto Scythian territory. Initially Darius planned to destroy the bridge behind him, adding the ships' crews and the bridge guard to the bulk of his army; but his advisers persuaded him to leave it intact. Instead, writes Herodotus, he took a leather thong and tied 60 knots in it, and gave it to the commanders of the rearguard. He ordered them to untie one knot each day after the army had marched. If he did not return by the time all the knots were untied, the rearguard was to sail for home; but until that day came they were to guard the bridge at all costs.

The Scythians were well aware of the menace which threatened them, and knew that they could not defeat such an overwhelmingly superior force in

nother face of the Kul Oba vessel shows two warriors nversing, both holding spears or javelins. The gorytos is early indicated on the left hip of the bare-headed spearman; s companion's shield is interesting, perhaps representing a ain leather covering over a wooden or wicker base.

GHT:
his third view of the Kul Oba vessel shows a warrior, his rytos exposed to us, binding a wounded comrade's leg.

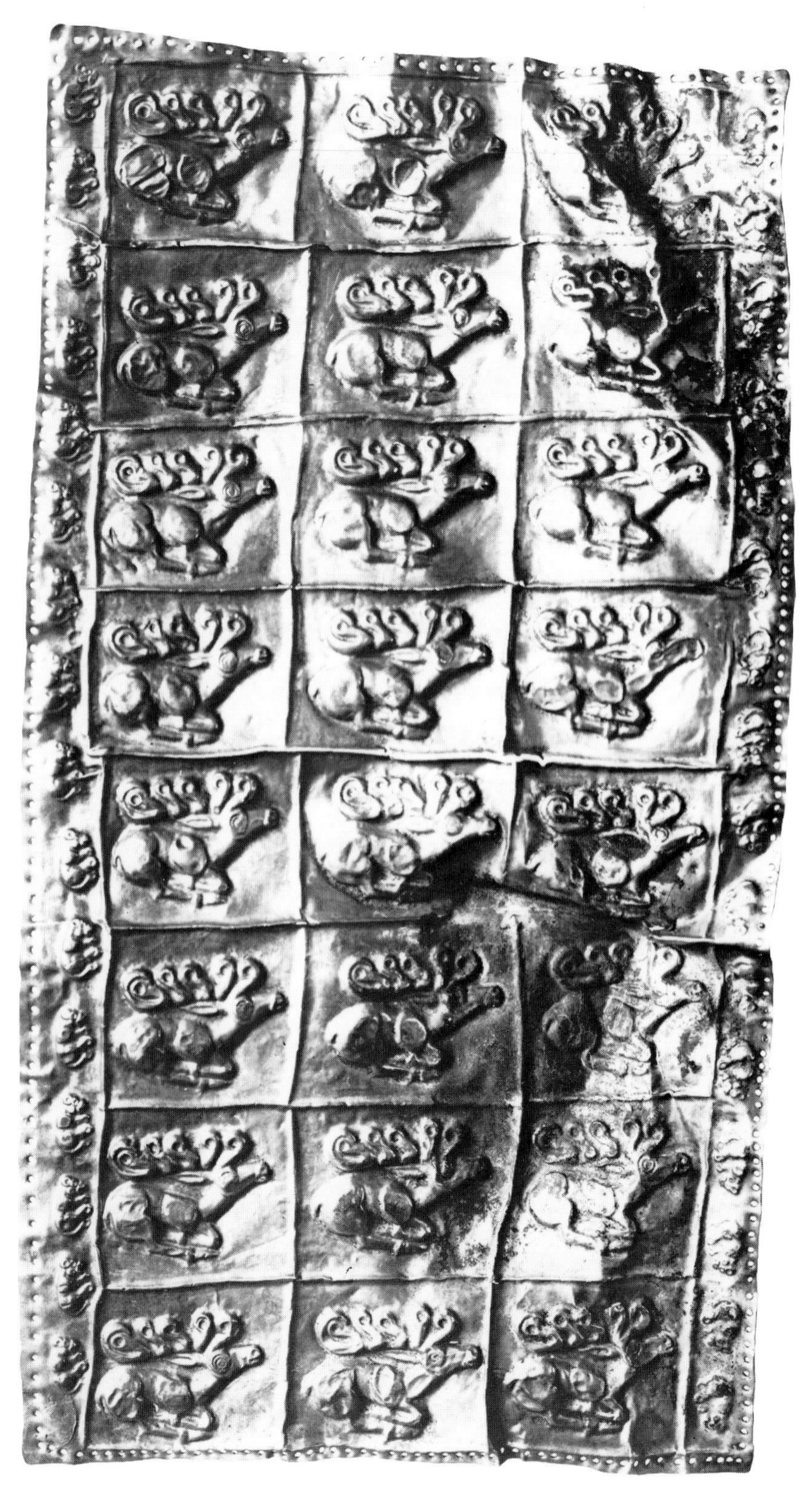

Gold gorytos facing plate from the 6th century Kelermes barrow, with a repeat pattern of deer motifs in the Scythian style. At this period only part of the gorytos was faced with decorative plates, and the disintegration of the leather structure leaves us with only an imperfect idea of the overall shape.

1: Scythian king, early 6th C. BC
2: Urartian nobleman, early 6th C. BC

A

1: Scythian warrior, late 6th/early 5th C. BC
2: Scythian warrior, 4th C. BC
3: Thracian warrior, 4th C. BC

B

1: Scythian warrior, 5th C. BC
2: Scythian nobleman, 4th C. BC

1: Armoured warrior, 5th C. BC
2: Armoured warrior, late 5th/early 4th C. BC

D

1: Scythian king, late 5th/early 4th C. BC
2: Armoured nobleman, 4th C. BC

E

1: Sindo-Meothic nobleman, 5th C. BC
2: Scythian nobleman, 5th C. BC
3: Scythian noblewoman, 4th C. BC
3
1
2
Angus McBride

F

1: Scythian king, 4th C. BC
2: Scythian queen and prince, 4th C. BC
3: Royal bodyguard, 4th C. BC

G

1: Young Scythian warrior, 4th C. BC
2: Scythian king, 4th C. BC
3: Nobleman, 4th C. BC
3
2
1
Angus McBride

H

en battle, or at least, not unaided. The council of aders turned to neighbouring tribes for help, nding out messengers to spread word of the nger, and to point out that the Persians would not content with conquering Scythia alone. But their ighbours' opinions were divided, and most re- sed to form an alliance. They justified this by inting out that the Persians were apparently sponding in kind to the Scythian invasions of the evious century. They declined to make enemies the Persians in such a cause, though determined defend themselves if the invaders proved to have der ambitions than punishing the Scythians.

Since even those forces which were promised to em would arrive too late to form a united front ainst the rapidly advancing Persians, the ythians had no choice but to fight on their own. t this time Scythia was divided into three separate ngdoms; the largest tribe provided the supreme ler, King Idanthyrsus, and his subordinate kings ere named Scopasis and Taxacis. Each led the st of his own tribe. At a council of war they agreed at it would be madness to oppose such a superior my in open battle, and that they must play for ne, hoping to wear the Persians out and forcing em to react to their strategy. They started to withdraw in the face of the invader, filling up wells and springs and burning off the grass as they went. The women, children and old people trekked north, driving the herds with them. Only the warriors and young women—who fought as equals—remained on the steppe.

The host was divided in two. The more mobile part, led by King Scopasis, was to head for the Danube to meet the invaders half way. They were to avoid direct contact, and to move east, keeping a day's march (perhaps 30 or 35 kilometres) ahead of the Persians, scorching the grazing and driving off the game as they went. The bulk of the Scythian army, led by Idanthyrsus and consisting of his own and Taxacis's troops, was to retreat parallel to the Persians and on their northern flank. Their two-fold task was to keep the enemy from turning towards the northern refuge of their people, and to channel the Persians always towards the burnt-out, water- less plains. The Scythians' goal was to let the enemy wear himself out on an exhausting pursuit-march

Gold facing plate for a gorytos recovered from the 4th century royal burial at Chertomlyk. The decoration, in the Classical style, shows an incident from Homer's 'Iliad': the visit of Achilles to the Isle of Skyros. Produced by a Greek craftsman to Scythian order, this piece has a border frieze of beasts and monsters of the kind found on so many surviving artefacts.

The world-famous gold pectoral found in the royal burial at Tolstaya Mogila, dating from the 4th century, is reconstructed on our Plate G. This is an enlarged detail from the pectoral, showing two Scythians—their bows and arrows always close at hand—apparently dressing a fleece.

across the steppes, and to attack him if a good opportunity arose.

We know from Herodotus that the Persian invasion force was mostly infantry, with some cavalry and a considerable train of baggage. The Scythians were all mounted, until perhaps the last stages of the campaign when footsoldiers of neighbouring peoples came to their aid. The weapons of the two sides were similar; the Scythians were probably the better archers, given their reputation as the finest bowmen of their time, and this gave them an obvious advantage in exactly the kind of running fight which they planned.

The Persians began their long march eastwards into the Scythian heartland. Their progress was slow. Historians and archaeologists have not agreed as to what route they followed, or how far they finally penetrated. Our principal source is not of great help on this point: Herodotus writes that the Scythians fell back through the territories of the tribes which had refused to help them, hoping to involve them in the war, thus implying th the Persians covered about 5,000 kilometres in on 60 days. This is clearly impossible, and the advan of a basically infantry army over such a distan would have taken three or four times as long even a forced pace. There were several major riv barriers—the Dniestr, Southern Bug, Ingul, I gulets, Dniepr, Don, and many smaller rive Besides the problems of terrain, the Persians we constantly in danger—and towards the end of the march, the very present danger—of harassi attacks, and were short of food, water and forag

The Scythians kept falling back, refusing to gi battle. By the time they reached the steppes north the Sea of Azov, the leather thong left with t commander of the Danube bridge guard had lc one third of its knots. There seemed to the Persia to be no end to the campaign, and its goals were far out of reach as ever. Not only were the Scythia undefeated; they grew stronger every day, as th fell back towards new forces joining them from t east. They had everything the invaders lacked- food, water and forage.

At last Darius decided to halt, and build a lar fortified camp on the northern coast of the Sea ov somewhere in the vicinity of the modern town Berdyansk. His purpose is not clear. He might ve planned to leave a strong garrison to pin down e enemy in that area while the mass of his army ntinued east; or he might have intended to wait his fleet to bring up provisions by sea. In any ent, the construction of the camp was never ished. Its walls were only half-built when Darius lled out for some reason, and resumed his pursuit the Scythians. Although the decisive battle he aved still eluded him, he had already lost a nsiderable number of men in skirmishes. It was en that Darius did something he had never done fore. He sent a messenger to King Idanthyrsus. 'Strange man', he said, 'why do you continually n away, when given the choice? If you think urself strong enough to contend with me, then p roaming, and turn and fight. If you confess urself to be weaker than I, you will have to stop yway, and open negotiations with your ruler, inging him earth and water as symbols of bmission'.

Herodotus reports that Idanthyrsus replied in these words: 'I have never run away for fear of any man. I am wandering, as I always wander in time of peace. You ask why I did not fight you at once. May I remind you that we have neither cities nor cultivated land of our own; since we are not afraid of our territory being ruined and plundered, we had no reason to fight you outright . . . Not will we, until we see fit. Instead of earth and water, I will send you other gifts, of the kind you deserve; and you will pay me dearly for calling yourself my ruler'.

Idanthyrsus kept his promise. The Scythians now began to adopt more aggressive tactics, harrassing and waylaying Persian foraging parties. The Scythian horsemen dominated the Persians in these skirmishes, sending Persian cavalry fleeing back in disorder into the ranks of their own infantry. Idanthyrsus had now committed the bulk of his personal forces, and detached Scopasis's horsemen westwards on an important mission. Since they had

Gorytos facing plate recently discovered in the Macedonian royal tomb—alleged by some to be that of Philip II—near the site of Vergina, northern Greece. This 4th century relic bears decoration which is believed to depict the fall of Troy.

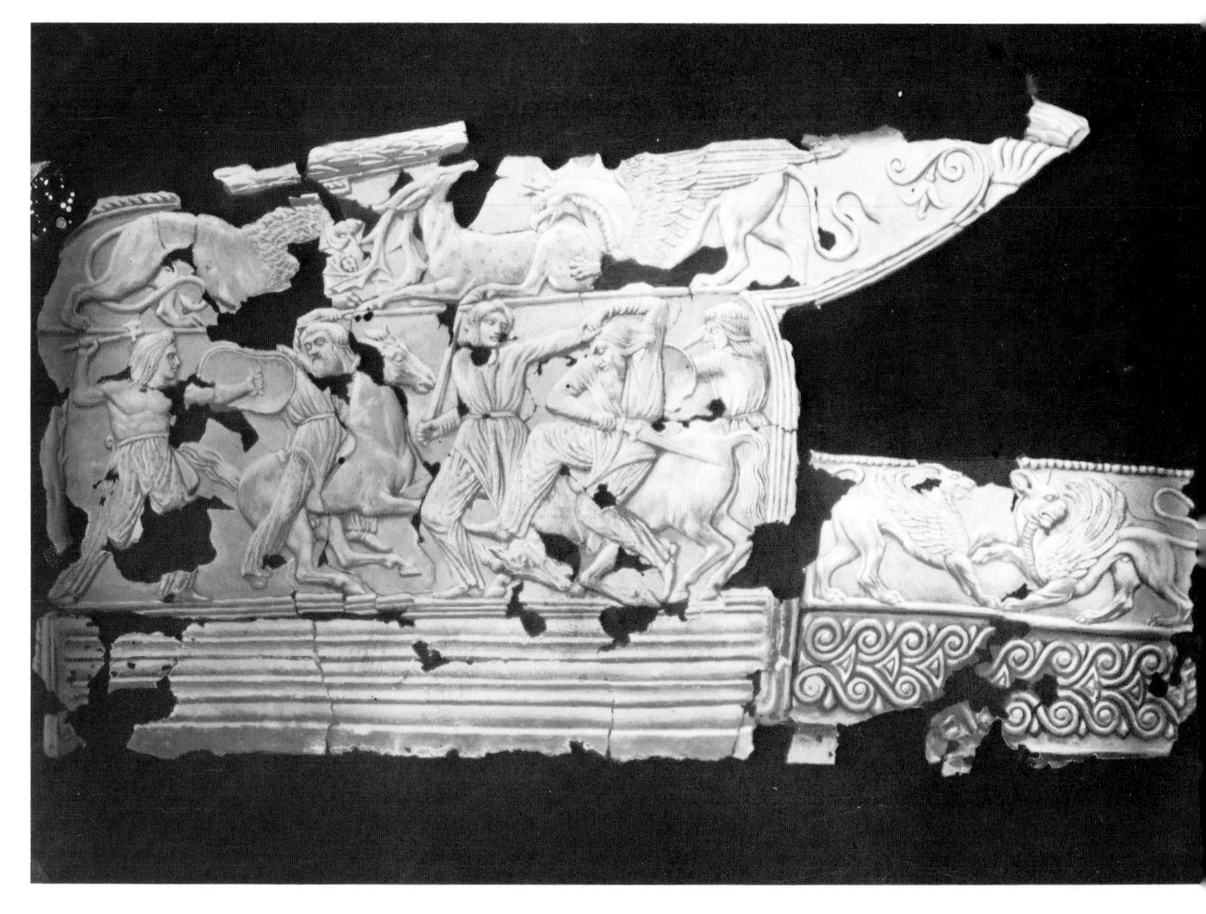

Gilded silver gorytos facing plate from the Solokha burial, showing a battle between young and old Scythian warriors; the legendary allusion is discussed in the text.

now begun to believe that the enemy could be defeated, the Scythians determined to cut them off by destroying the Danube boat-bridge. Scopasis reached the Danube, and parleyed with the Greek vassal force who guarded the bridge. It is reported that he accepted an assurance that the Greeks would dismantle the bridge, but rode eastwards again without waiting to see it done, and that the Greeks broke their word and kept the bridge intact.

Now Idanthyrsus sent Darius the gifts he had promised: strange gifts for the great king—a mouse, a frog, a bird, and five arrows. Darius chose to interpret these as meaning that the Scythians accepted unconditional surrender: they were offering him their land (for mice live in the earth and eat grain, like men); their water (for frogs live in water); their horses (represented by the bird, symbolising the means of their freedom and their most valuable possession); and were laying down their arms before him (the arrows). A courtier interpreted the message in a different way, howev 'If you Persians do not fly away like the birds, hide in the earth like mice, or leap into a lake li frogs, then you will never see your homes again, b will die under our arrows.' The continuing course the campaign soon convinced Darius that t second interpretation was the right one.

One day he received word that the enemy seem about to offer him the decisive battle upon which l hopes rested. Even though his army was weaken and tired out, he was still confident in its ability overwhelm the Scythians in pitched battle. T adversaries ranged themselves for combat—but soon transpired that far from seeking battle, t Scythians had thought of a new way to show th disregard for the great king. As the armies faced o another, a frightened hare started up from the gra between the battle lines—and the Scythians hors men whirled away to pursue it. The message w unmistakable to the Persians: 'These people hold in utter contempt.' Darius decided, at long last, salvage his army while he could still escape from t boundless steppes of Scythia.

)ne night fires were banked high in his camp; the ɩnded and those unable to travel fast were left ind, with the tale that the army was going out to ːe the Scythians to battle. But instead Darius led ɔrced march back towards the Danube, abanɩing his wounded and all his train in an attempt ·each the bridge while he still could.

ⱥ second Scythian attempt to persuade the ·eks to destroy the bridge seemed to have ːceeded, but it was only a feint; the bridge was y opened by the distance of a bow-shot. The sians and Scythians missed one another in the kness of night, and the next morning Darius ɩnd with relief that his means of escape was still ɩct. He led his surviving forces into safety, ɩing a large number dead on the steppes without ɩ having come to battle.

'he victory over Darius brought the Scythians a ɩutation for invincibility, which is confirmed in ɩny Greek and Roman accounts.

Scythian Warcraft

ːient sources offer us only the most scarce and ɩeral information on the conduct of war by the ɩthians. Even less is known about the turbulent century than about the Persian invasion. One ɩg is clear, however; the Scythians expanded .r influence westwards and north-westwards. A ɩ of this is the famous cache of arms found near ːaszkowo in Poland; these are probably the ve-goods of a leader killed in the assault on a ress there, and laid to rest with a panoply of ch a sword, a golden fish decoration from a ·ld, and richly decorated horse-trappings sur-ː.

ɩ little more is known about Scythian campaigns inst the Thracians. After Darius was driven k with shame, the Scythians started to press r western neighbours, and continued to do ːhroughout the 5th and 4th centuries BC. The ɩnts of the second half of the 4th century are the st interesting; it was at this time that Macedonia an to grow strong under the leadership of Philip Thrace found herself between the devil and the p blue sea: on her west, Macedonia, and beyond Danube, Scythia. The high king of the

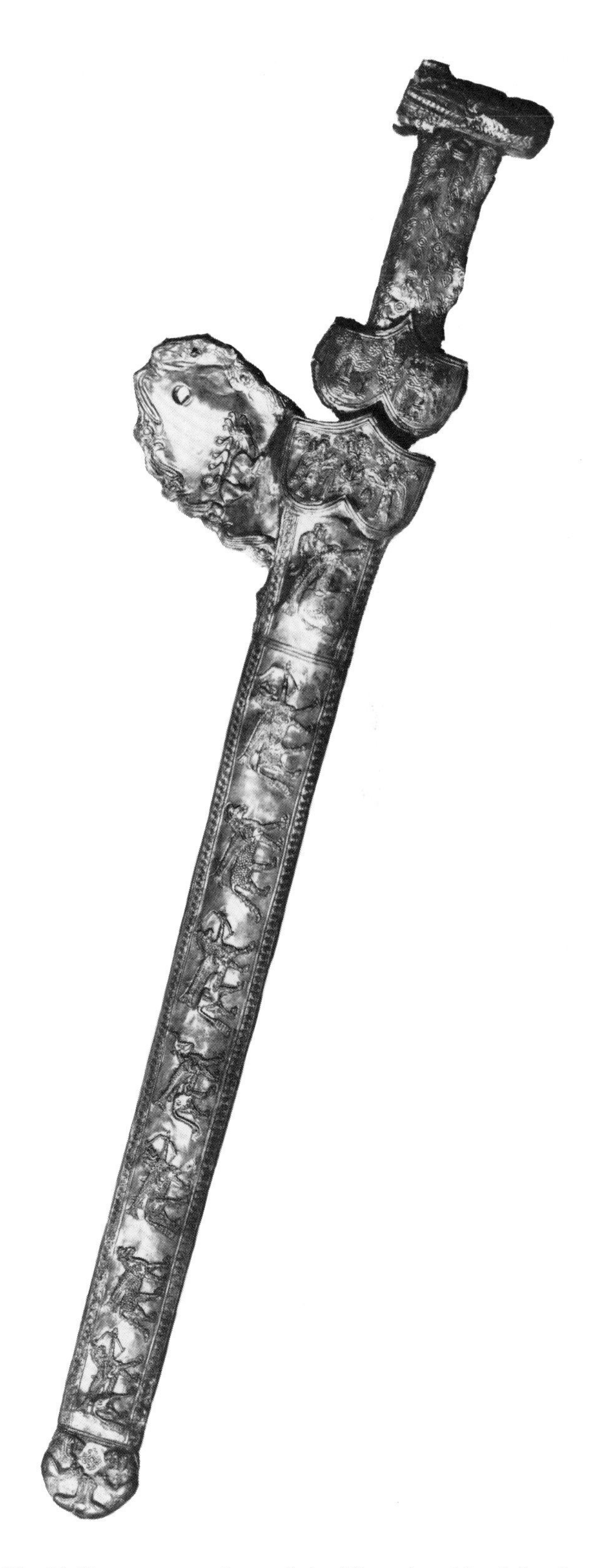

The highly ornamented sword, its hilt and scabbard faced with stamped gold plate, found in the 6th century Kelermes burial; this is one of the two oldest Scythian swords known. Note the straight-sided grip and simple crossbar pommel. The protruding 'ear' is pierced for the slinging thong.

Scythians, the aged and cunning Atheas, had long wished to add the lands of the Thracians to his range. The long diplomatic struggle for influence in Thrace ended in 339 BC when the 90-year-old king was killed and his army defeated by the Macedonians.

Yet this defeat, though bitter, could not have ruined Scythian power. Only nine years later Zopyrion, a general sent by Alexander the Great, invaded Scythia with 30,000 men with the goal of conquering Scythia's ally Olbia. He met with utter defeat, and his army left its bones on the steppes near Olbia. To our frustration, no details have come down to us of the course of these two battles or tactics used.

The only more or less detailed account of battle fought by the Scythians comes to us fr Diodorus Siculus, who describes events on Scythi eastern borders in the late 4th century BC. 310–309 BC Scythia took a part in the confl between heirs of ther Bosphoran king, Paerisad The throne went to the king's eldest son Satyr but his brother Eumeles contested the clai Fleeing from the capital, Panticapaeum, he tc refuge with the Thataeans who lived along Kuban River in the Northern Caucasus. T

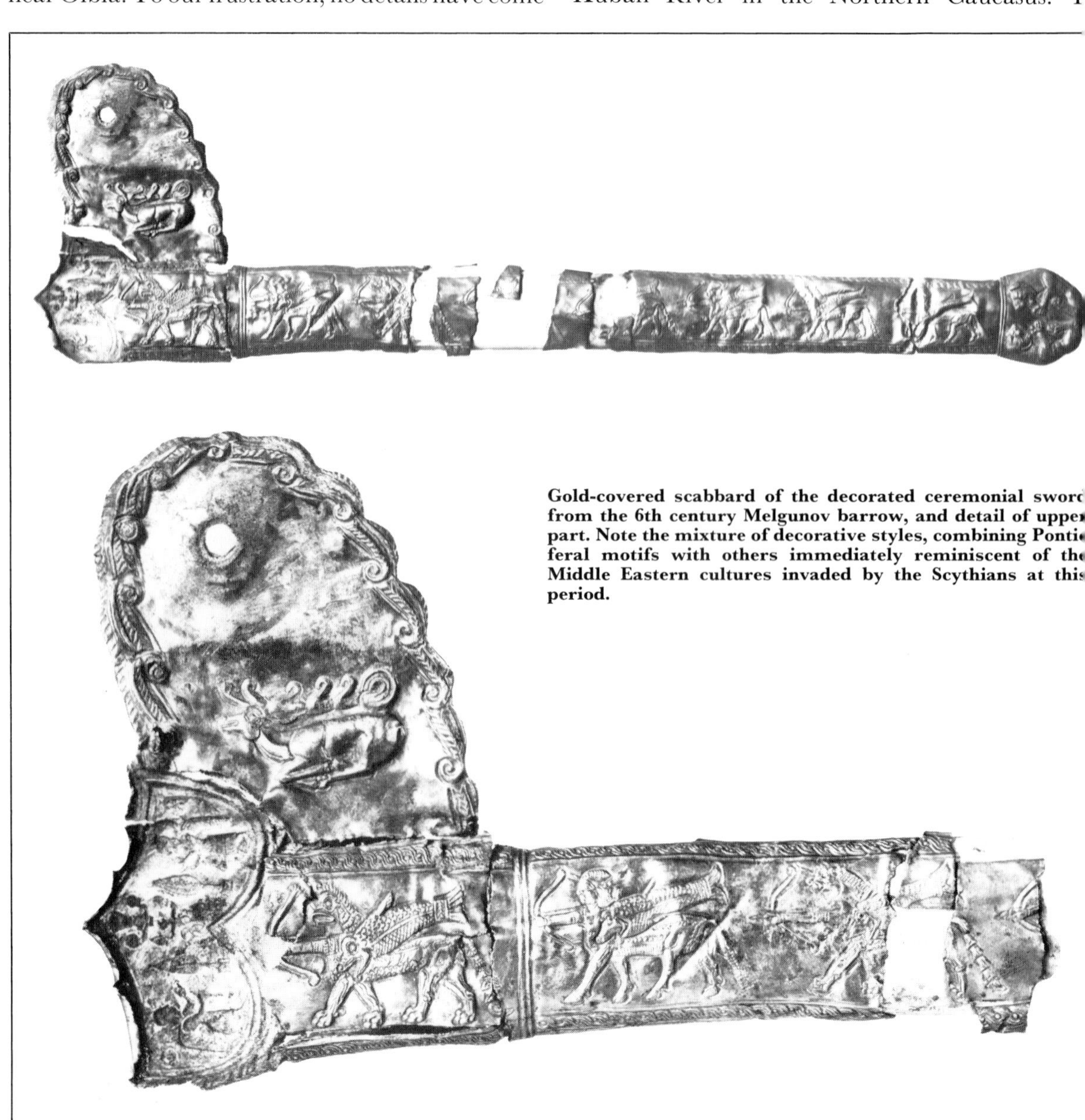

Gold-covered scabbard of the decorated ceremonial sworc from the 6th century Melgunov barrow, and detail of uppe part. Note the mixture of decorative styles, combining Ponti feral motifs with others immediately reminiscent of th Middle Eastern cultures invaded by the Scythians at thi period.

hataeans had been made vassals of the Bosphoran ngdom not long before, and seized this opportnity to free themselves. They sided with Eumeles, d their king, Aripharnes, led a large army of ,000 horse and 20,000 foot to resist the pursuing rces of Satyrus.

Satyrus had an impressive army himself, with ,000 Greek and as many Thracian mercenaries; it likely that the Greeks were equipped as hoplites, d that the Thracians were lightly-armed peltasts. he bulk of the Bosphoran army, however, was ade up of Scythians—10,000 horse and 20,000 ot—since Scythia had long maintained ties with e kingdom of Bosphorus. Note the ratio of horse foot in the opposing armies; in Satyrus's force, 1 2, and in the Thataean army, 1 to 1. No other my of Classical antiquity is recorded as having ch numbers of cavalry; even Alexander the Great, ho paid great attention to his mounted arm, never lded more than 1 to 5 or 6 cavalry to infantry. his high cavalry content, at times exceeding the fantry, characterised the armies of northern ntic peoples in the Scythian period.

Satyrus fielded a total of 34,000 men and umeles and the Thataeans 42,000; apart from his erall superiority, the pretender had 20,000 horse the Scythians' 10,000. From what we know it ems that the weaponry of each side was largely entical, though archers were probably more umerous among the Scythians.

The Scythians marched up-country into the hataeans' territory, and were obliged by the lack forage to take with them a train of several indred wagons. When they reached the River hatis they found the enemy drawn up on the far nk to receive them. Satyrus made a bold decision: succeeded in crossing the river, made a fortified mp out of his wagon train, and drew up his troops nmediately in front of it. He stationed Greek ercenaries, presumably in their usual phalanx rmation, on his right flank, supporting that wing ith Thracian peltasts and a troop of Scythian orse. Another detachment of the cavalry and fantry held the left wing. In the centre Satyrus led s select shock-troops: the bulk of the Scythian orse, including the heavily-armoured élite.

Diodorus has little to tell us about the Thataean der of battle. On the whole it was similar to that of e enemy: Eumeles was on the left flank with a

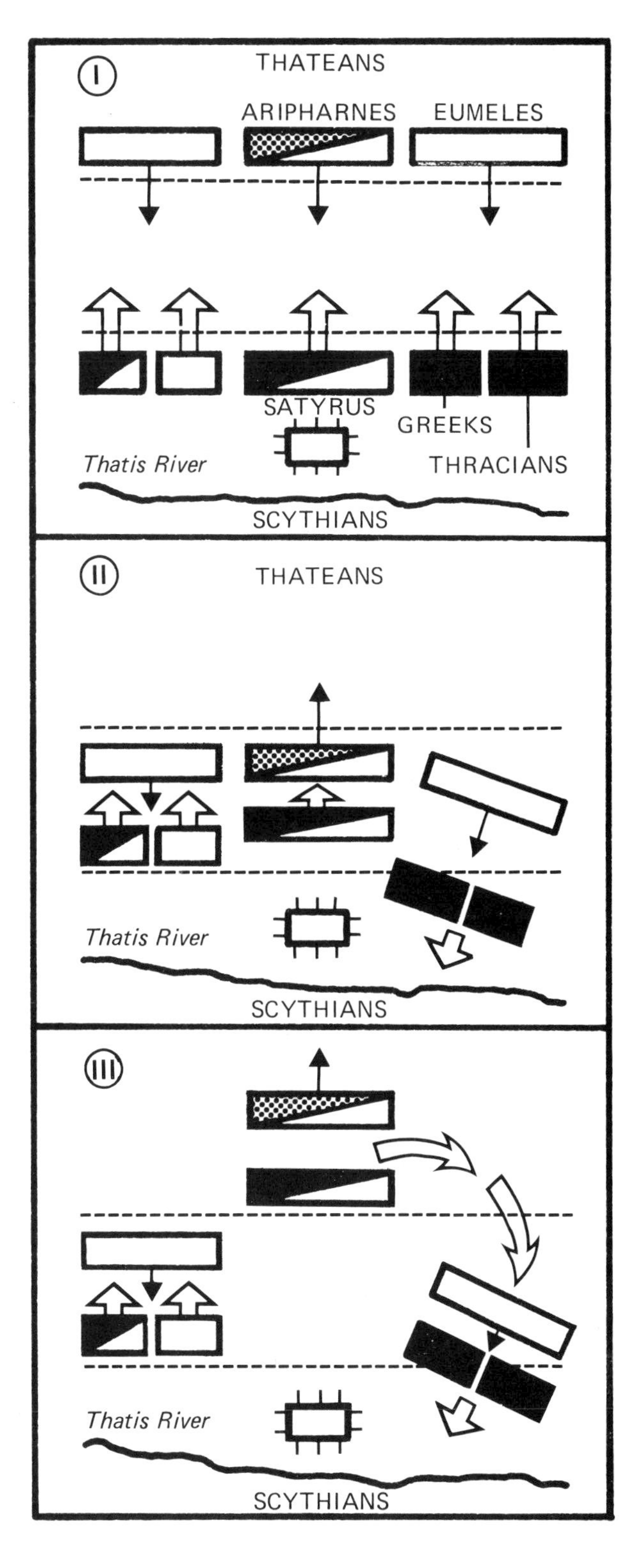

The battle of the River Thatis, 310 or 309 BC. (I) The armies ranged for battle. (II) Satyrus leads the Scythian heavy horse in a successful charge on the Thataean centre, while his right wing gives way before the enemy cavalry led by Eumeles. (III) After putting the enemy centre to flight, the Scythian horse regroups and swings round to take the Thataean left wing in the rear.

force of cavalry to engage the Greek and Thracian mercenaries, and infantry faced infantry on both wings. Aripharnes was in the centre with the bulk of his cavalry, headed by heavy units.

Both sides suffered heavy losses as soon as the battle began. At first Eumeles enjoyed some success on the left flank, and the Greeks and Thracians wavered. In the centre the Bosphoran king led his Scythian horse forward, smashing Aripharnes's cavalry in a short meeting engagement; they penetrated the enemy's second line, and soon put them to flight. The final blow was delivered by Satyrus leading the Scythians in a charge into the rear of Eumeles's command, ending his temporary advantage on the left wing and routing his forces. The surviving Thataean troops fled, and took refuge in a fortress.

This battle underlines the high combatant value of Scythian horse, achieved by firm discipline and the indisputable authority of its leaders as much as by the individual skills of the warriors. The Scythian cavalry managed to retain its cohesion after breaking through the enemy lines; regrouped in the thick of the battle; and decided the day by a second charge in another direction at a second body of the enemy. Very few armies of antiquity were capable of that manoeuvre.

The 4th century BC marked the peak of Scythian prestige, and the beginning of a steady decline. Gradually the Sarmatian tribes, who were related to the Scythians, began to cross the Don and encroach upon their territory. The Scythian range shrank, year by year, for reasons which are lost to us. For some time they lingered in 'Scythia Minor'—the area of the lower Dniepr and the Crimea. They yielded the northern Pontic steppes to the Sarmatians; and two hundred years after their victory on the Phatis River they disappeared altogether as a significant force in history. They leave us the mystery of their rise and their fall; and a haunting legacy of superb metalwork, chased with vigorous and beautiful images from the days of their barbaric splendour.

The Plates

Commentary by Dr. M. V. Gorelik

A1: Scythian king, early 6th century BC

This reconstruction of a Scythian king late in th period of the Middle Eastern invasion is based o finds in the barrows near Kelermes in th Kuban; the shield was found in a barrow nea Stanitsa Kostromskaya. The king's iron ax and the hilt and scabbard of his sword, have gol sheathing, chased in the Scythian style by Urartia (Armenian) craftsmen. He is also armed with spear, and a bow and arrows in a goryt (combined bow and arrow case) decorated with chased gold face plate; the gold clasp is probably Greek workmanship from Asia Minor. The ca bronze helmet is of Scythian origin; the bod armour, of iron scales sewn to leather, is typical Scythian. The iron facing of the shield is unique: i the centre is a panther motif in Scythian 'anim style'. From the girdle, decorated with gold orna ments, is slung a golden sup. The gold decoration bridle and breast-strap is Scythian work; the sadd cloth, of a type common to all Iranian peoples, typical of the Scythians.

A2: Urartian nobleman

These weapons and armour are based on finds fro the excavation of the Urartian fortress Teishebaini. The helmet is typical of this cultur the armour is of bronze scale construction. H carries a chased bronze quiver, and an iron swor with ivory hilt decoration. His clothing is recor structed from wall-paintings and ceramics fro Urartu.

B1: Scythian warrior, late 6th/early 5th century BC

Reconstructed from finds in barrow no. 3 nea Khutor Popovka in Poltava province. The wea ons are an iron sword, a battle-axe and a spear. Th body-girdle, from the barrow near the village Shchuchinka, is very wide, and is made fro several rows of iron scales and long curved plat sewn to leather. The facing of the shield is uniqu thick plates of bone are sewn to a wooden backin Note the scalps of enemies decorating the bridl and a fresh scalp slung at the waist—after Her

omplete contrast, a very plain and functional iron sword ı a bronze hilt, the pommel shaped into two 'talons'. This found in a Scythian burial dated to the 5th century, in the epr area.

us. The saddle cloth is the flayed skin of a dead my.

Scythian warrior, 4th century BC
is prosperous warrior is reconstructed from finds barrow no. 493 near the village of Ilyintsi in nitsa province. The leather armour has a toral and appliqué plates of bronze. The sword t is made of small bronze strips; the greaves are work of a Greek master. Weapons include a bow l arrows, a javelin and a spear. The fur or fleece ic is from pictorial work on the pectoral from lstaya Mogila barrow; the hairstyle, untypical of Scythians, is taken from representations on gold plates from Kul Oba barrow. He stands over his fallen Thracian enemy; it is believed that scalps were still taken at this time.

B3: Thracian warrior, 4th century BC
The costume is reconstructed from Greek vase-paintings and from Thracian metalwork objects; the weapons are from archaeological finds, and include the *kopis* or *machaira* sword, typical of this region and period. Note fox-fur cap, long ornamental cloak, and boots trimmed with goat's hair.

C1: Scythian warrior, 5th century BC
A rich warrior, reconstructed from finds at barrow no. 2 near the village of Volkovtsi in Poltava province. The leather body armour with attached scales resembles that worn by a warrior on the famous comb from the Solokha barrow. The typical shield has iron strips sewn to each other and to the wooden base with wire, and is edged with leather. Again, the girdle is of very narrow bronze strips. Note the length of the sword. He also carries a bow and arrows in a gorytos, a spear, a dagger and a javelin. The clothing comes from the pictorial decoration of the cup from Gaimanova Mogila barrow. The bridle was found complete in the tomb.

C2: Scythian nobleman, 4th century BC
This *nomarchos* or 'prince' is reconstructed from finds in barrow no. 1 near the village of Volkovtsi. The helmet is of Greek 'Attic' style. Bronze scales from the breast armour and bone scales from the shoulder-pieces were found in the tomb; the body defences are completed by a girdle of bronze plates. The warrior had a pointed iron axe, its haft decorated with a spiral gold band; a spear, a javelin, and a bow and arrows. The gorytos was decorated with gold plates, and others were sewn to the sleeves of the tunic. The gold-decorated bridle was found almost complete; the breast-strap of the harness had bronze decorative plates.

D1: Fully-armoured warrior, 5th century BC
Reconstructed from archaeological data from barrow no. 3 near Staikin Verkh in the forest-steppe zone (Northern Ukraine). The heavy armour, made of iron scales sewn to leather, gave an excellent defensive covering to the whole torso, the

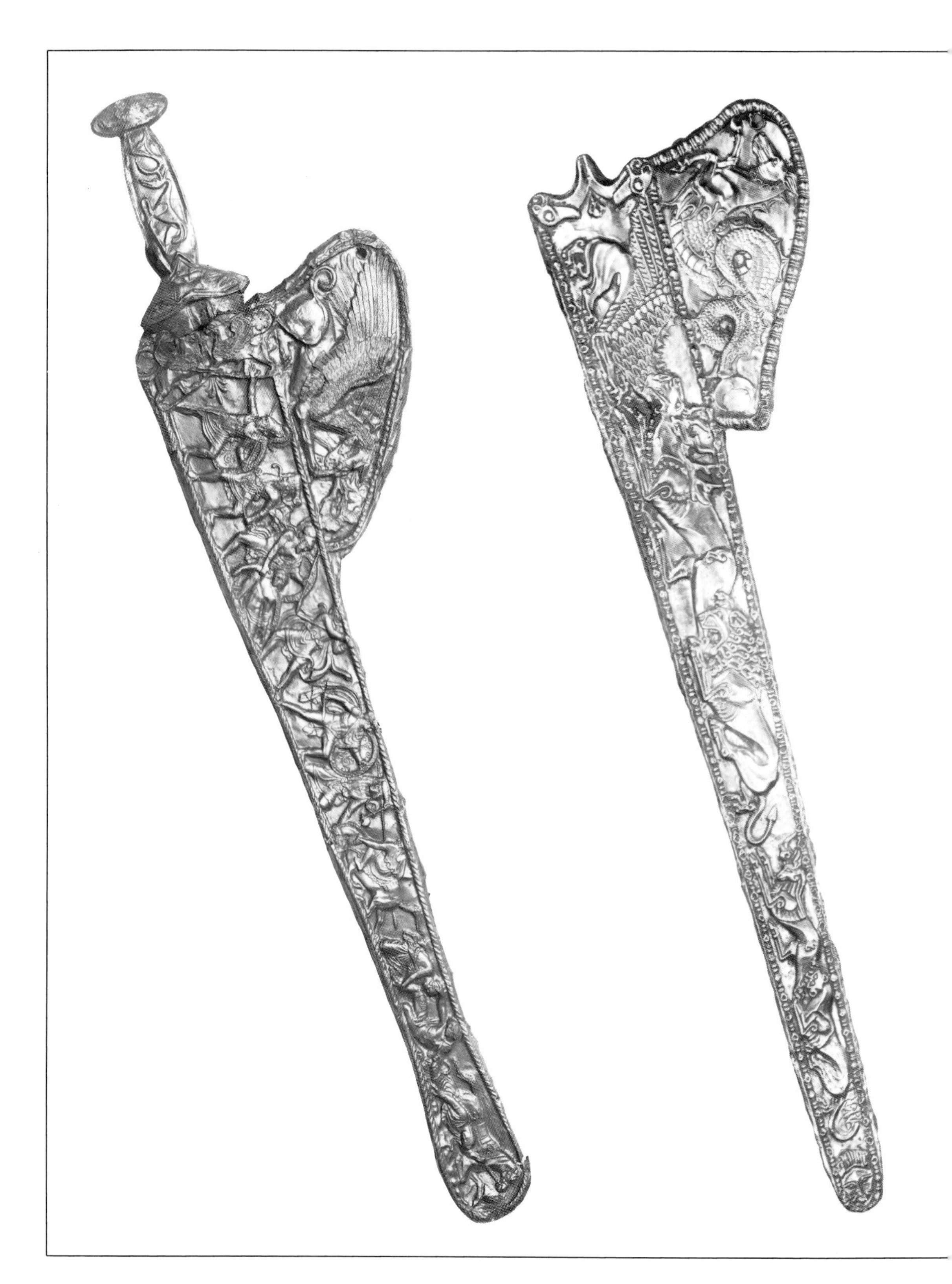

4th century ceremonial sword, the hilt and scabbard gold-plated; note the oval pommel and tapering grip more typical of this period. The decoration combines Scythian animal motifs with a battle scene in the Classical style including figures in both Greek and Scythian costume.

This ceremonial scabbard from the Kul Oba royal buri decorated entirely with real and mythical beasts; compare pure feral style of the animals near the tip, with the Greek-looking execution of the 'sea-horse' on the protru 'ear'.

ns and the legs. We take the shield from the lokha comb, the Kul Oba vase, and other ırces. A comprehensive set of weapons is carried: ord, battle-axe, spear, and bow and arrows.

: *Fully-armoured warrior, late 5th/early 4th century BC* though believed to be a rank-and-file fighting ın, this warrior reconstructed from finds in the rrow near Novorozanovka village wears a beautiiron scale body armour of Scythian workmanp, which was found almost intact. The helmet s the form of a cap, with scales covering the skull d iron strips on the ear-flaps and neck-guard. ɔte the usual bronze-strip girdle. The leggings ach to bronze buttons, fixed to the inner surface the body armour, by means of special loops. A ɔically comprehensive set of weapons is carried.

: *Scythian king, late 5th/early 4th century BC* constructed from finds in the Solokha barrow, s warrior-king wears full battle armour. The lmet is a re-worked Greek piece, of Attic, alcidian or Corinthian manufacture. The body mour is of iron scale construction, with short eves. Note the Greek bronze greaves, which have upper part cut off—perhaps in order to make it sier to control the horse with the knees. The shield vered with iron strips is taken from the Solokha mb. Note the cup, of Greek workmanship in a ythian decorative style, slung from the girdle. ıe sword hilt and scabbard are covered with ded silver plate, decorated by Greek craftsmen th a battle-scene of Scythians, beasts and griffons. ıe bronze mace thrust into the bronze-strip girdle ıs a sign of the highest social rank as well as a apon. The set of golden bridle decorations is tremely rich, with many frontal and nasal urines; usually we find only a single figurine. The of bronze decorations on the breast-strap of the rness is typically Scythian. All harness decations were of Scythian workmanship, rather an foreign. The front edge of the soft saddle has pliqué golden triangles, and decorative gold ates are sewn to the clothing and footwear. The rque is the work of a Greek master. Note also the de bracelets, another mark of royal status.

: *Fully-armoured Scythian nobleman, 4th century BC* constructed from the pictorial detail on the

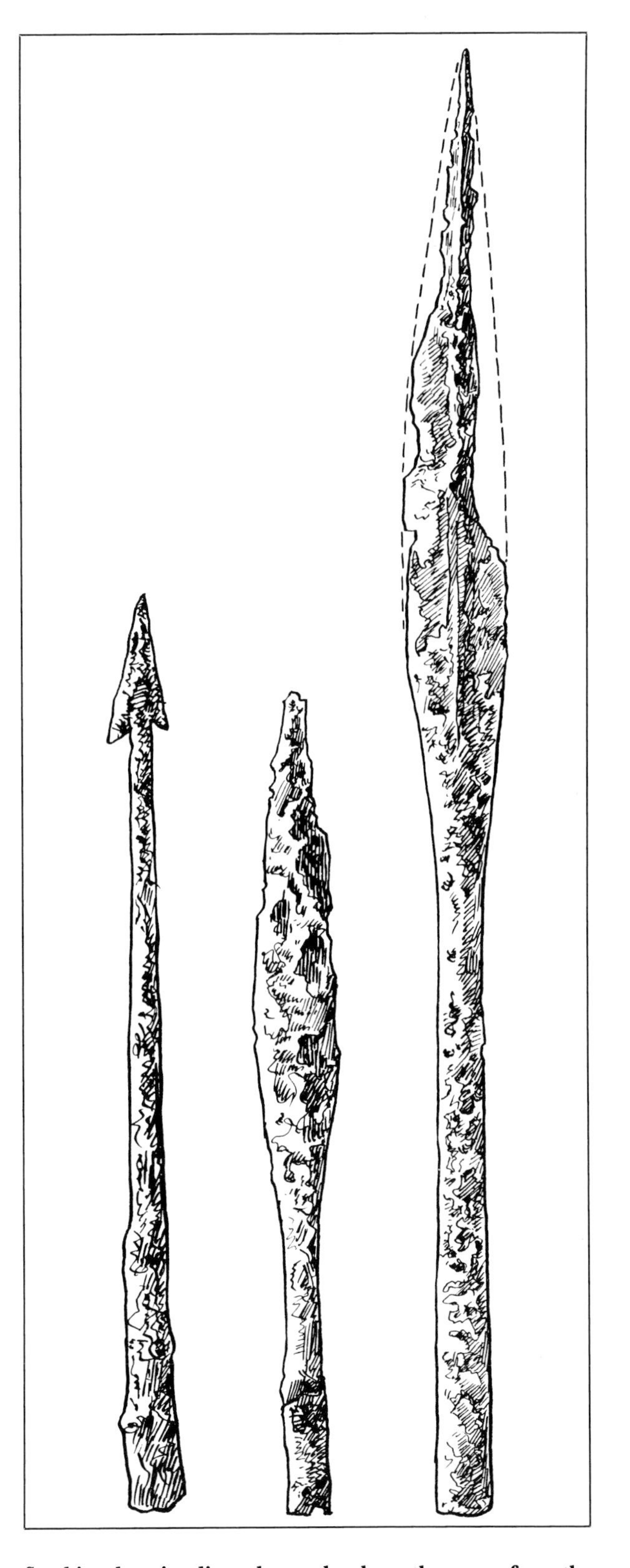

Scythian dart, javelin and spear heads, as they came from the ground; the longest is more than 70cm from socket to tip. The dart invites immediate comparison with the later Roman *pilum*, and Frankish *angon*. These were unearthed from various 6th to 4th century burials.

Side view, and head detail, of the gold-sheathed axe from the 6th century mound at Kelermes. The exposed iron blade, now deteriorated, was decorated in the same style as the goldwork.

golden plate, of Scythian workmanship, found in Geremesov barrow. The bronze helmet of Chalcidian style, manufactured in Italy, has had a scale neckguard added by local smiths. The heavy scale body armour of local workmanship, with long sleeves and thigh defences, is supplemented by a triangular pectoral—we have not yet found one of these pieces, but we may see it depicted on later Sarmatian finds. The greaves have been deliberately modified, the knee-pieces being cut off and replaced by separate domed defences: a logical modification of heavy infantry armour for mounted use. The same sources show us a unique example of scale breast armour for the horse. The shield, fac with iron strips and mounted with a bronze figure a fish, was found in a barrow near Ordzhonikidze Dniepropetrovsk province. The gorytos is fac with a superbly chased golden plate depicting eagle, worked by Greek craftsmen to Scythi order; this was found in Dört Oba barrow in t Crimea.

F1: Sindo-Maeotic noblemen in full armour, 5th cent BC

This impressive figure is reconstructed from a stat now in Krasnodar Museum. The bronze helm manufactured in northern Italy, was found ne Stanitsa Dakhovskaya in the Kuban, close to t site where the statue was found. The scale-fac shield is taken from the Solokha comb, and from ɜnt find in Kherson province. The leather body ıour had pauldrons and long sleeves; note that skirt is much longer at the rear than at the front. ɜ pauldrons and upper breast are decorated with ;e bronze plates in the animal style, which bably combine defensive, aesthetic and magical ctions. We have archaeological evidence for the of iron strips sewn to the sleeves. The breast and t of the armour are covered with iron scales. The ue shows us clear representations of a long rd, and a dagger in a tasselled sheath; one can see a whip with two tassels, and a gorytos taining arrows and two bows.

Scythian nobleman, 5th century BC

ɜ defensive armour was found in the tombs of the n of Nymphaeum in the Crimea—the helmet in row no. 1, the remainder in barrow no. 6—and ow in the Ashmolean Museum, Oxford. The orted bronze helmet of Illyrian style was re-ked by a Scythian armourer, who cut off the k-guard and attached it at the brow to form a k. Part of a shoulder-piece of Classical-style her armour, with attached bronze scales, was nd in one tomb. The body armour was dec-ted with a bronze plate in the form of an elk's d on the breast. The girdle consisted of 'dagged' nze strips. The Scythian greaves are of typical struction: strips of bronze are attached together to the leather base with wire. The sword, whose ed hilt and sheath combined Scythian and ek decorative elements, was found in Ostraya gila barrow near the village of Tomakovka. The golden decorative work on the quiver-section of gorytos, and the truncated cone of gold which ns to be a decorative fixture for scalps, were nd in the Crimea in a barrow near Ilyitchëvo.

Scythian noblewoman, 4th century BC

ɜ women's tombs found near Ordzhonikidze ded several examples of war-gear for women riors. There was no body armour; the costume ıbined female elements—a 'tiara' headpiece, a collarless tunic with a long skirt—with male ısers. Typical features were a bow and arrows in orytos which had a sheath for a knife let into the ɜ, a spear and a javelin. Swords are rare in female ıbs, only three being known. A mirror, as shown ɜ slung to the girdle, is invariably found.

Two angles of the head, and one of the butt, of the bronze mace found in the 4th century royal tomb known as the Solokha mound.

G: Scythian king and his retinue on the march, 4th century BC

The costume of the king, G1, his queen and their little son, G2, are reconstructed from archaeological finds in the royal barrow of Tolstaya Mogila near Ordzhonikidze. The king wears an iron scale corselet with shoulder-pieces, the edges rimmed with gold, and the breast decorated with a chevron of stamped leather painted red and covered with gold foil. An iron Scythian girdle and bronze Greek greaves complete the defensive armour. The mace, once again, signifies the highest social rank. The sword, with chased gold decoration, is the work of Greek masters following Scythian designs. The silver plate facing the gorytos has appliqué decorations of gilded bronze in the Scythian animal style. The handle of the whip has a spiral gold band, and a tassel of gold beads at the head. The costume is lavishly decorated with gold plates, and on the king's breast can be seen the world-famous pectoral, the work of a Greek goldsmith.

The queen wears a gown, shawl and headdress decorated with the same kind of gold appliqué-work; the position of these plates in the tomb enabled archaeologists to reconstruct the form of the costume. Note the mirror slung at the waist. The little prince already wore a torque at the neck and a royal bracelet on his arm.

The king's mount has a bridle decorated with chased plates of gilded silver, of Greek workmanship, and a breast-strap with typically Scythian bronze ornaments.

The king's bodyguard ride with him, under a standard consisting of horsetails flying from a bronze capital mounted on a pole. The nobleman, G3, wears an armour found in a barrow near Dniepropetrovsk; his silver-decorated bridle, and the breast strap with a protective apron of bronze plates, come from Krasny Kut barrow. A field camp of Scythian travelling vans can be seen in the background.

H1: Young Scythian warrior, 4th century BC

A young warrior of humble birth brings the head of his first-slain enemy to his king, and is rewarded with a ritual cup of wine. He is armed with the usual bow and arrows in a gorytos. He has the head of a Macedonian military leader in his hand, and has stripped his enemy of his armour and weapons; a

5th century Scythian sculpture of a warrior king. Th ancient figures, which were originally raised on the top of finished burial mounds, have been found on several sites

eco-Macedonian helmet and greaves were ıd in a hoard near Oloneshti in Moldavia, a ld in Kurdzhipsky barrow in the Kuban, and ments of a sword at Olbia. Note the warrior's ; hair—this could only be cut after he had killed first enemy.

Scythian king, 4th century BC

chief of one of the tribes that acknowledged the ıority of the Bosphoran kingdom, he is reconcted from finds at the Kul Oba royal barrow on Kerch peninsula in the Crimea. A number of ron scales of the body armour were gilded; the le was of gilded iron strips, and Greek greaves plete the armour. Note the rich golden decive work on the headgear and clothing; the torque, bracelets and rings, all of Greek workmanship; the hilt and sheath of the sword covered in Greek goldwork, and the knife and whetstone set in gold. The shield, of wood and leather, is decorated with a golden deer—again, Greek work made to Scythian order.

H3: Young nobleman, 4th century BC

This royal bodyguard of high birth has an armour of Graeco-Scythian type, combining bronze scales and strips, which seems to be the work of Bosphoran armourers. This kind of Scythian 'splinted' greaves were found in barrow no. 4 of the 'Seven Brothers' group in the Kuban. The sword is taken from one found in a barrow at Bolshaya Belozerka near Zaporoshye.

ıian coin bearing the name and likeness of King Atai—ously, 'Ateas' or 'Atheas' in the Greek form—who died in e against the Macedonians at the age of 90. It is acteristic that he should be shown on horseback, bow in . The Scythians attached enormous importance to the e herds upon which their culture was founded. It is ved that there were three main types of horse. The st, with a height to the withers of about 144 to 150cm (14¼ ¾ hands) was relatively scarce, and is mainly represented ery rich burials; it can be compared to an Arab ughbred, and was apparently used as a battle charger by the nobility. The most frequent type was smaller, about 140cm (13¾hh) to the withers; this was an all-purpose breed for battle, work, and draught, and was rather smaller and lighter than our present-day saddle horse. The smallest, about 130cm (12¾hh) to the withers, was bred largely for its meat—a favourite Scythian dish. Pictorial sources suggest that the Scythians preferred to ride stallions. Mummified horses found at Pazyryk, and some cases of well-preserved horse burials on the European steppes, suggest that the preferred colour was 'red', and it seems that horses with white markings were bred out.

Notes sur les planches en couleurs

Toutes les planches sont fondees sur des découvertes archéologiques en Union Soviétique. Voir les légendes en langue anglaise pour les localités des tumulus applicables dans chaque cas.

A1 Casque en bronze et corselet en fer, à écailles monté sur cuir, de confection typiquement scythe. Noter le gorytos caractéristique: carquois et gaine à arc combinés—et la coupe pendue à la ceinture. **A2** Noble arménien, reconstitué d'après des fresques des ruines de Urartu, et des témoignages archéologiques.

B1 Remarquer la large ceinture protégeant l'abdomen; les scalps des ennemis à la bride et à la ceinture, et la peau écorchée d'un ennemi abattu utilisée comme couverture de cheval. Le bouclier est unique en son genre, garni de bandes en os. **B2** L'armure en cuir renforcée de plaques de bronze appliquées est scythe, mais les jambières sont grecques. Style de coiffure inhabituel, extrait d'images sur objets d'art en métal trouvé à Kul'Oba. Il s'agit d'un chef fortuné. **B3** Costume thracien reconstitué à partir de témoignages pictoraux sur des vases, etc.

C1 Riche guerrier portant une armure en cuir renforcée d'écailles et un bouclier en bois à bandes de fer. La longue épée n'est pas typique. **C2** Ce prince porte un casque grec Attic, des vêtements ornés de plaques d'or, et une armure à renfort en os sur les épaules, particularité peu ordinaire. Le gorytos, comme d'habitude, comporte des plaquettes en or sur la surface extérieure, décoré dans le style 'de chasse' des Scythes.

D1 Armure en écailles de fer complète, peu commune; noter la panoplie typiquement riche: épée, hache, javelot, arc et flèches. **D2** Une autre découverte archéologique admirable nous a permis de reconstituer cette armure en écailles complète; les jambières sont accrochées à des boutons en bronze à l'intérieur des basques de la tunique. Le casque en forme de casquette est renforcé d'écailles et de bandes de métal montées sur cuir.

E1 Roi guerrier en tenue de bataille complète: casque grec remanié, jambières grecques, harnais de cheval exceptionnellement très décoré, bouclier et corselet du type scythe, et armes et équipements superbement décorés par des artisans grecs mais dans le style scythe. Les bracelets, et la masse d'armes passée dans la ceinture, sont des attributs de royauté. **E2** L'un des gardes du corps nobles du roi; ici aussi, le casque et les jambières, de fabrication grecque, ont été modifiés par des artisans scythes. La protection pectorale du cheval par armure en écailles est unique en son genre. Le gorytos, découvert en Crimée, est de qualité particulièrement fine; une fois de plus, le style est scythe mais le travail est grec.

F1 Noter l'armure en cuir exceptionnelle, peinte et dorée; le casque de fabrication italienne, découvert dans le Kuban; le fouet garni de glands, et le gorytos avec deux arcs. **F2** Des objets découverts en Crimée, mais se trouvant actuellement en Angleterre, sont notamment: casque illyrien à protège-nuque découpé et refixé à l'avant, comme visière, par un armurier scythe. Ici, les jambières sont typiquement scythes. **F3** Les articles servant à la guerre sont rares mais pas inconnus dans les tombeaux des femmes, mais en pareil cas, des épées n'ont presque jamais été découvertes. Des pièces typiques sont le gorytos à fourreau de couteau incorporé à la plaque frontale et le miroir pendu à la ceinture, à la façon dont les hommes portaient parfois des coupes.

G Magnifiques costumes royaux d'un roi, de sa reine et de leur petit garçon, découverts dans des tombeaux royaux près d'Ordzhonikidze. L'ensemble comprend des éléments de travail local—décoration à motifs de chasse, et plaquettes d'or cousues sur les vêtements—il faut signaler aussi la contribution de maîtres-artisans grecs. L'ornement pectoral du roi est célèbre dans le monde entier en tant que découverte tombale. Derrière la famille royale se tient son garde-du-corps avec un étendard à queue de cheval.

H Un jeune guerrier d'humble naissance apporte comme tribut au roi la tête de son premier ennemi abattu: un officier macédonien. Il reçoit en récompense une coupe de vin rituelle. Le roi et son garde du corps noble portent divers articles d'origine mixte scythe et grecque. Des accessoires guerriers macédoniens capturés figurent parmi plusieurs précieuses découvertes.

Farbtafeln

Alle Rekonstruktionen basieren auf Funden in der Sowjetunion; Sieh Tafelbeschreibungen in englischer Sprache für Namen und Lage der jewe Grabhügel.

A1 Bronzehelm und eiserner Schuppenbrustpanzer (mit Lederunterlag typischer skythischer Ausführung; beachte den charakteristischen Goryt (binierter Bogen- und Pfeilköcher) soie die vom Gürtel hängende Trinkschal Uratäischer Vornehmer, rekonstruiert nach Wandmalereien in den Ruine urartäischen Festung Tejsebaini und archäologischen Funden.

B1 Beachte den breiten Kampfgurt, der den Unterleib schützt, Skalpe Feinden am Zaumzeug und Gürtel und die abgezogene Haut eines getö Feindes als Pferdedecke sowie den einmaligen Schutzschild (mit Knochenpl besetzt). **B2** Die Lederrüstung mit aufgesetzten Bronzeplatten ist skythisch Beinschienen jedoch griechisch. Ungewöhnlicher Haarstil, nach Bildern Metalplättchen von Kul Oba. Dies ist ein wohlhabender Krieger. Thrakischer Krieger, rekonstruiert nach griechischer Vasenmalerei un chäologischen Funden.

C1 Reicher Krieger, Lederrüstung mit aufgesetzten Schuppen tragend un einem typischen hölzernen Schutzschild mit aufgesetzten eisernen Platten lange Schwert ist weniger typisch. **C2** Dieser Fürst trägt einen attischen H mit Goldplatten verzierte Kleidung und eine Rüstung mit ungewöhnl Schulterverstärkung aus Knochenschuppen. Der Goryt hat, wie bei Vorneh üblich, eine Goldplatte auf der Aussenfläche, im skythischen Tierstil verz

D1 Ungewöhnlich kompletter Fund einer eisernen Schuppenrüstung; beachte den typisch reichhaltige Bewaffnung—Schwert, Axt, Lanze, Bogen Pfeile. **D2** Ein anderer hervorragender archäologischer Fund ermöglicht es diese volle Schuppenrüstung zu rekonstruieren; der Beinschutz ist in Bro nöpfe an der Innenseite des Panzerhemdes eingehakt. Der Helm ist wie phrygische Mütze geformt, mit auf Leder montierten Schuppen und Eisen ten als Ohren- und Nackenschutz.

E1 Ein König in voller Kampfausrüstung, einschliesslich eines umgearbei griechischen Helmes, griechischem Beinschutz, einem ungewöhnlich reichh verziertem Pferdegeschirr, einem Schild und Kampfgurt von skythischem Waffen und Ausrüstung hervorragend verziert von griechischen Handwerk jedoch in skythischem Stil. Die goldenen Armreifen und der im Gürtel steck Streitkolben sind Zeichen des königlichen Rangs. **E2** Vollgerüsteter skythis Fürst; wiederum sind Helm und Beinschienen aus griechischer Herstellung skythischen Handwerken modifiziert worden. Der schuppengepanzerte Bru chutz für das Pferd ist ein einmaliger Fund. Der Goryt, auf Krim gefunden, ist besonders hoher Qualität; wiederum ist der Stil skythisch, jedoch die Ausfüh griechisch.

F1 Beachte die ungewöhnliche Lederrüstung, schuppenbesetzt und verzier Italien hergestellter Helm, im Kubangebiet gefunden; eine mit Qua geschmückte Peitsche; und ein Goryt mit zwei Bögen. **F2** Funde von der K nunmehr in England, schliessen einen illyrischen Helm mit abgeschnitte Nackenschutzein, der vorne als Schirm von einem skythischen Waffenschr wieder angebracht wurde. Die Beinschienen hier sind typisch skythisch. Kriegsausrüstung in Frauengräbern ist ungewöhnlich, jedoch nicht unbek obwohl Schwerter in solchen Fällen sehr selten gefunden werden. Typisch Goryt, hier mit einer eingebauten Messerscheide in der Frontplatte; und Spiegel am Gurt in der Art und Weise, wie Männer manchmal Trinksch trugen.

G Herausragende Ausstattung eines Königs, seiner Königin und deren klei Sohn, nach Königsgräbern in der Nähe von Ordzhonikidze. Die Ausstatt beinhaltet sowohl einheimische Arbeit—Tierstil-Verzierung und auf die K dung aufgenähte Goldplättchen—als auch Auftragsarbeit von griechisc Meistern. Der Brustschmuck (pektorale) des Königs ist ein weltberühr Grabfund. Hinter der königlichen Familie ist seine Leibwache mit e Pferdeschwanzstandarte.

H Einer junger Krieger von niedriger Herkunft bringt der Kopf seines ersten ihm getöteten Feindes—ein mazedonischer Offizier—zu seinem König und v mit einem feierlichen Becher Weines belohnt. Der König und seine vorneh Leibwache tragen zahlreiche Gegenstände gemischten skythisch-griechisc Ursprungs. Erbeutete mazedonische Waffen (wie hier abgebildet) wurder verschiedenen skythischen Horten und Gräbern gefunden.